Proud is joy: Exploring LGBTQ+ Identity in Today's World and Conquering Confidence in a World Obsessed with Labels

Nicole J Barker

TABLE OF CONTENT

DEDICATION

This book is dedicated to all those who strive to embrace their true selves and stand proud in their LGBTQ+ identity. May you find the strength to conquer confidence in a world that tends to focus too much on labels. Remember, your uniqueness is your power and your joy. Embrace it, celebrate it, and never be afraid to show the world who you truly are. Stay proud, stay strong, and always remember that you are deserving of love, acceptance, and happiness.

INTRODUCTION

Welcome to "Proud is Joy: Exploring LGBTQ+ Identity in Today's World and Conquering Confidence in a World Obsessed with Labels."

Have you ever felt like you didn't quite fit in? Like there was a part of you that society didn't understand or accept? If so, you're not alone. Many people have experienced the struggle of navigating their identity in a world that often feels judgmental and unwelcoming.

But here's the thing: your identity is something to be celebrated, not hidden away. In this book, you will get to explore what it means to be LGBTQ+ in today's society, the complexities of sexual orientation, gender identity, and the myriad of labels that society tries to place on people.

But more than that, we'll discover the joy that comes from embracing who you truly are. Because being proud of your identity isn't just about acceptance – it's about finding joy in your authenticity, and empowering yourself to live your truth boldly and unapologetically.

So whether you're just beginning to explore your identity or you've been on this journey for years, this book is for you. It's a roadmap to self-discovery, a source of inspiration, and a reminder that you are worthy of love, acceptance, and pride.

Let's embark on this journey together and discover the joy that comes from being proud of who you are.

Chapter 1

A Brief History of LGBTQ+ Rights

Picture this: it's a hot summer day in June, and the streets are lined with rainbow flags and energetic crowds. You can feel the excitement in the air as people of all ages, races, and identities gather together to celebrate love and equality. But the journey to this moment of pride and acceptance was not an easy one. The LGBTQ+ community has faced centuries of oppression and injustice in their fight for equal rights. Let's take a trip back in time and explore the brief history of LGBTQ+ rights.

The term "LGBTQ+" stands for lesbian, gay, bisexual, transgender, and queer/questioning. Before the 20th century, these identities were rarely talked about, let alone accepted. Throughout most of history, same-sex love and gender-nonconformity were seen as taboo and even punishable by death. In ancient Greece, same-sex relationships were common and even celebrated, but it wasn't until the Roman Empire that homosexuality was criminalized. This set the stage for centuries of persecution and stigma towards the LGBTQ+ community.

Fast forward to June 28, 1969, in New York City's Greenwich Village. Police raids on gay bars were common at the time, and a raid at the Stonewall Inn sparked a six-day long uprising by members of the LGBTQ+ community. This event, known as the Stonewall Riots, is considered the birth of the modern LGBTQ+ rights movement. It led to the formation of LGBTQ+ activist groups and sparked the first Pride marches.

Throughout the 1970s and 1980s, the LGBTQ+ community continued to fight for visibility and equal rights. In 1973, the American Psychiatric Association removed homosexuality from its list of mental disorders, a huge step towards destigmatization. However, the community faced a devastating setback with the outbreak of the AIDS epidemic in the 1980s. The government's slow response and lack of support for the LGBTQ+ community further highlighted the discrimination and neglect faced by the community.

But the 1990s saw a turning point in the fight for LGBTQ+ rights. The enactment of hate crime laws and anti-sodomy laws being declared unconstitutional were significant victories for the community. The world also witnessed the first openly gay government official, Harvey Milk, being elected to public office in 1977. Sadly, his term was cut short due to his assassination, but his legacy continues to inspire and empower.

The 21st century has seen a rise in public support and legal recognition for the LGBTQ+ community. In 2000, Vermont became the first state to legalize civil unions for same-sex couples, and in 2015, the U.S. Supreme Court legalized same-sex marriage nationwide. This was a major milestone in the fight for LGBTQ+ rights, but the battle for equal rights continues.

Today, the LGBTQ+ community still faces discrimination, hate crimes, and unequal treatment in many parts of the world. However, the courage and determination of activists and allies have brought about incredible progress and change. Pride celebrations have become a global phenomenon, and more and more countries are recognizing and granting equal rights to the LGBTQ+ community.

As we celebrate Pride month, let us remember and honor the brave individuals who fought for the rights we enjoy today. Let us also recognize that there is still work to be done in the fight for equality and acceptance for all identities. Stand with the LGBTQ+ community and continue to strive for a world where love is love and all individuals are treated with dignity and respect.

Congratulations, you've now traveled through the brief history of LGBTQ+ rights. Keep this journey in mind and continue to educate yourself and others on the struggles and triumphs of this community. Together, we can create a more inclusive, understanding, and accepting world for all. Happy Pride!

The origins of the modern gay rights movement, dating back to 1969 and the Stonewall Riots.

Imagine living in a time when being gay was not only considered taboo, but it was also illegal. A time where discrimination and hate towards the LGBTQ+ community was not only socially acceptable, it was the norm. This was the reality for many individuals in the United States in the 1960s.

It was during this time that the modern gay rights movement began to take shape. The catalyst for this movement dates back to June 28th, 1969, at the Stonewall Inn in New York City. The Stonewall Inn was a popular bar for the LGBTQ+ community, often frequented by individuals who were rejected and marginalized by society.

On that fateful night, a routine police raid was conducted at the Stonewall Inn. However, this time, the patrons of the bar decided to fight back. They had reached their breaking point – tired of being harassed and mistreated for simply being who they were. The raid sparked a series of protests and demonstrations that lasted for days, known as the Stonewall Riots.

The Stonewall Riots were not the first or only forms of resistance by the LGBTQ+ community. However, it marked a turning point in the fight for gay rights. It ignited a flame that burned across the nation, as individuals came together and demanded their rights and recognition.

In the years following the Stonewall Riots, the gay rights movement gained momentum and expanded its reach. In 1973, the American Psychiatric Association removed homosexuality from its list of mental illnesses, a significant step in destigmatizing being gay.

In 1978, the rainbow flag was introduced as a

symbol of pride for the LGBTQ+ community, thanks to artist Gilbert Baker. It provided a sense of unity and visibility for a community that had long been pushed to the fringes of society.

The 1980s and 1990s brought both progress and setbacks for the gay rights movement. The AIDS crisis brought attention and recognition to the LGBTQ+ community, but at a high cost. Many individuals lost their lives to the disease, and the government's slow response only added fuel to the fire of anger and frustration.

Despite the challenges faced by the LGBTQ+ community in the following decades, there were also significant victories. In 1996, President Bill Clinton signed the Defense of Marriage Act, defining marriage as a union between a man and a woman. However, this ignited a call for equality, leading to the landmark Supreme Court case of Obergefell v. Hodges in 2015, which legalized same-sex marriage nationwide.

The modern gay rights movement continues to

evolve and make strides towards equality and acceptance. In recent years, the focus has shifted to issues such as transgender rights and discrimination against the LGBTQ+ community in the workplace.

Legacy organizations such as the Human Rights Campaign, GLAAD, and the Trevor Project work tirelessly to advocate for LGBTQ+ rights and provide support for those in need. Pride events, first held in commemoration of the Stonewall Riots, are now celebrated globally as a way to honor the LGBTQ+ community and its progress.

The origins of the modern gay rights movement may have started with the Stonewall Riots, but it continues to this day. The fight for equality and acceptance of the LGBTQ+ community is an ongoing journey, one that requires constant vigilance and perseverance. It is a journey that should be understood and celebrated by all, as it represents the fight for the basic human rights that every individual deserves.

The impact of Hitler on the suppression of LGBTQ+ rights

As you walk down the streets of Berlin, you can't help but feel a sense of fear and apprehension. The once vibrant and diverse city has now been transformed into a controlled and regimented society, all thanks to one man - Adolf Hitler.

Hitler and his Nazi party rose to power in Germany during the 1930s, with a vision of creating a pure Aryan society. Along with their hatred for Jews, they also targeted other minority groups, including the LGBTQ+ community. This resulted in the systematic suppression and persecution of LGBTQ+ individuals, leaving a long-lasting impact on their rights and freedoms.

One of the first things Hitler did upon becoming Chancellor of Germany was to eradicate the existing LGBTQ+ rights that were put in place during the Weimar Republic. He considered homosexuality to be a threat to the Aryan race and believed that it undermined the traditional family unit. He referred to it as 'degenerate' and 'unnatural', and passed laws to ensure its eradication from society.

The infamous Paragraph 175 of the German Penal Code, which criminalized homosexuality, was strengthened under Hitler's reign. This resulted in the arrests and imprisonment of thousands of LGBTQ+ individuals, who were often subjected to torture and inhumane treatment. Many were sent to concentration camps, where they were forced to wear pink triangles, a symbol of their supposed 'deviance' and were subjected to the same brutality as Jews.

Furthermore, Hitler's regime enforced strict gender roles and expectations, with women expected to conform to traditional female norms and men to exhibit hyper-masculine behavior. This left no room for anyone falling outside these strict binaries, and those who did were deemed as a threat to the Nazi ideology.

The impact of Hitler's suppression of LGBTQ+ rights was not just limited to Germany. Many other countries saw an increase in discrimination and violence against the LGBTQ+ community, as Hitler's beliefs spread beyond Germany's borders. This resulted in the persecution of LGBTQ+ individuals in occupied countries as well.

Even after Hitler's defeat and the fall of the Nazi regime, the impact of his policies on the LGBTQ+ community continued. Many of those who survived the concentration camps faced further persecution and were not granted reparations for the injustices they had suffered.

It took decades for LGBTQ+ rights to be recognized and protected in Germany and other countries affected by Hitler's regime. The scars of his systematic suppression are still present today, with many LGBTQ+ individuals and communities facing discrimination and hatred due to the lingering effects of his policies.

Therefore , Hitler's influence on the suppression of LGBTQ+ rights cannot be understated. He created a society where being different was seen as a threat, and this unjustified fear and hatred continue to impact the lives of LGBTQ+ individuals to this day. It is a reminder of the dangers of allowing one person's ideologies and prejudices to dictate the lives of others and serves as a cautionary tale for the importance of protecting the rights and freedoms of all individuals, regardless of their sexual orientation or gender identity.

The suppression of early gay rights movements, such as the one in Berlin, Germany.

Imagine living in Berlin, Germany in the early 20th century, where homosexuality was widely viewed as a moral and social taboo. Homosexuality was not only considered a sin, but it was also a criminal offense that could land you in prison, or even worse, subjected to cruel medical experiments and persecution. This was the harsh reality for the LGBTQ+ community during this time, who were constantly living in fear and facing suppression from the government and society.

The suppression of early gay rights movements in Berlin, Germany can be traced back to the 19th century. During this time, homosexuality was seen as a form of "degeneracy" and was heavily stigmatized. This belief was further fueled by the writings of renowned psychiatrist Richard von Krafft-Ebing, who categorized homosexuality as a mental illness in his popular book "Psychopathia Sexualis". As a result, homosexuality was seen as a threat to the moral fabric of society, and any attempts to challenge this notion were met with severe consequences.

Despite the oppressive environment, Berlin became a haven for the LGBTQ+ community in the early 1900s, with its vibrant nightclubs and underground scene. This attracted many queer individuals from all over Germany and Europe, who found solace and a sense of belonging in this liberal and open-minded city.

However, the growing presence of the LGBTQ+ community did not go unnoticed by the authorities. In 1871, the German Reichstag passed Paragraph 175, a law that criminalized same-sex sexual acts. This law remained in effect until 1969, making Germany one of the last countries in Europe to decriminalize homosexuality.

The suppression of gay rights movements in Berlin was also aided by the rise of the Nazi party in the 1920s. Under Hitler's regime, LGBTQ+ individuals were targeted and persecuted, with the infamous pink triangle being used to identify and shame them in concentration camps. Many LGBTQ+ activists and advocates were arrested and imprisoned, while their organizations and publications were shut down.

One of the most notable cases of suppression during this time was the "Institut für

Sexualwissenschaft" (Institute for Sexual Research), a pioneering research institute co-founded by Magnus Hirschfeld. The institute was dedicated to studying and advocating for sexual diversity and it attracted many queer individuals, including artists, writers, and intellectuals. However, in 1933, the Nazis ransacked the institute, burned its archives, and publicly humiliated and shamed its members. This event marked a turning point for LGBTQ+ rights in Germany and it would take decades to rebuild and regain the progress that was lost.

The suppression of early gay rights movements in Berlin not only had devastating effects on the lives of LGBTQ+ individuals but it also had long-lasting consequences on their visibility and representation in society. The oppressive environment forced many queer individuals to lead secret and isolated lives, and the absence of a united movement made it difficult to challenge discrimination and demand equal rights.

However, despite the challenges and setbacks,

the suppression of gay rights movements in Berlin also sparked a resilience and determination among the LGBTQ+ community. Many activists and organizations continued to fight for their rights and contributed to the gradual shift towards acceptance and understanding in Germany. Today, Berlin is recognized as one of the most LGBTQ+ friendly cities in the world, with a plethora of LGBTQ+ bars, clubs, and events that celebrate and embrace diversity.

With that been said , the suppression of early gay rights movements in Berlin, Germany was a dark period in history that caused immense harm and suffering to the LGBTQ+ community. It serves as a reminder of the consequences of discrimination and the importance of standing up for what is right, even in the facc of adversity. It is a testament to the strength and resilience of the LGBTQ+ community, and a reminder that their fight for equality and acceptance is far from over.

The significance of the Stonewall Riots in sparking the modern movement

As you walk down Christopher Street in New York City's Greenwich Village, you can't help but feel a sense of history and empowerment. This street, with its bustling cafes and rainbow flags, holds a significant place in the LGBTQ community. It was there, in the early hours of June 28th, 1969, that the Stonewall Inn, a popular gay bar, became the site of a historic event that would ignite the modern movement for LGBTQ rights. Let's take a journey back in time to understand the significance of the Stonewall riots and how they continue to resonate with the community today.

At the time, homosexuality was still considered a criminal offense in most parts of the United States. The LGBTQ community faced constant discrimination and harassment from the police, who often raided gay bars and arrested patrons simply for their sexuality. The Stonewall Inn was a haven for the community, as one of the few places where they could gather and be themselves without fear of persecution.

But on that fateful night in June, everything changed. The police arrived for a routine raid, but this time, the LGBTQ community refused to back down. What started as a routine arrest quickly turned into a full-blown uprising. Patrons of the Stonewall Inn, along with members of the community who had gathered outside, fought back against the police, refusing to be treated as criminals. The rioters, mostly made up of transgender women, people of color, and homeless youth, threw anything they could find at the police, from bottles to bricks.

The riots continued for several days, with protesters chanting 'Gay power!' and 'We're here, we're queer, get used to it!' The community, who had been silenced and marginalized for so long, finally found their voice and were determined to be heard. The Stonewall riots were a turning point, where the LGBTQ community stood up for their rights and demanded to be treated with dignity and respect.

In the aftermath of the riots, LGBTQ activists organized and formed groups such as the Gay Liberation Front and the Gay Activists Alliance, advocating for gay rights and equality. The first Gay Pride rallies were also held to commemorate the anniversary of the Stonewall riots, with the first being held on June 28th, 1970.

The Stonewall riots were a pivotal moment in history, not just for the LGBTQ community, but for the entire world. It sparked a global movement for LGBTQ rights, with people coming together to fight for equality and acceptance. The events at the Stonewall Inn on that summer night in 1969 not only ignited a fire within the LGBTQ community but also brought attention to the ongoing discrimination and violence faced by the community.

Today, the Stonewall Inn is a national historic landmark, serving as a reminder of the bravery and resilience of the LGBTQ community. Its significance, however, goes beyond its physical location. The Stonewall riots have inspired generations of activists and continue to be a symbol of hope and courage for those fighting for LGBTQ rights around the world.

 As you walk away from Christopher Street, you carry with you the knowledge of the Stonewall riots and the immense impact they had on the modern movement for LGBTQ rights. Remember, the fight for equality is far from over, but thanks to the bravery of those who stood up that night in June, we are one step closer to a more inclusive and accepting world.

Key figures in the movement, including Marsha P. Johnson and Sylvia Rivera.

As you wander through the streets of New York City, you may come across a statue depicting two fierce and powerful women. These women are Marsha P. Johnson and Sylvia Rivera, two key figures in the LGBTQ+ rights movement who fought tirelessly for equality and the rights of marginalized communities.

Marsha P. Johnson, born in 1945 in New Jersey, was an African-American transgender woman, drag queen, and activist. She moved to New York City in the 1960s and became a part of the vibrant LGBTQ+ community in Greenwich Village. Marsha was known for her outspoken personality, vibrant fashion sense, and her pivotal role in the Stonewall uprising of 1969.

On a hot summer night in June, police raided the Stonewall Inn, a popular LGBTQ+ bar in NYC. Marsha and other activists fought back against the unjust treatment and harassment from the police, sparking a 6-day-long protest and eventually leading to the birth of the modern-day LGBTQ+ rights movement. Marsha's leadership and bravery during the Stonewall uprising cemented her as a vital figure in the movement.

Following the Stonewall uprising, Marsha co-founded the Street Transvestite Action

Revolutionaries (STAR) with her close friend Sylvia Rivera. Together, they created a safe haven for homeless and transgender youth in New York City. Marsha and Sylvia's tireless work within STAR provided shelter and support for marginalized youth who faced discrimination and violence from society.

Sylvia Rivera, born in 1951 in New York City, was a Latina transgender activist and a fierce advocate for LGBTQ+ rights. At a young age, she was abandoned by her father and shortly after, her mother passed away, leaving her to fend for herself at the age of 11. Sylvia was forced to live on the streets, where she faced discrimination, violence, and poverty due to her gender identity.

In 1963, at the age of 12, Sylvia met Marsha P. Johnson and they quickly became close friends. Together, they navigated the tough streets of New York City and stood up for each other and their community. It was this friendship that sparked a powerful partnership, as they both shared a dream of creating a safe space for LGBTQ+ youth.

In addition to her work with STAR, Sylvia was a vocal activist for transgender rights. She co-founded the Gay Liberation Front and participated in the Christopher Street Liberation Day March, a precursor to the NYC Pride March we know today. Sylvia's influential advocacy and leadership helped pave the way for the inclusion of transgender rights in the LGBTQ+ movement.

Despite the discrimination and challenges they faced, Marsha and Sylvia never wavered in their fight for equality and the rights of marginalized communities. They were proud of their identities and used their voices to bring attention to the issues faced by LGBTQ+ individuals, especially people of color and transgender individuals. As a result of their bravery and determination, they have become icons and role models for future generations of activists.

Today, their legacy lives on through various organizations and initiatives that continue to fight for LGBTQ+ rights. The Marsha P. Johnson Institute, founded in 2015, honors Marsha's memory and advocates for the protection and rights of Black trans people. Likewise, the Sylvia Rivera Law Project, founded in 2002, provides legal services and support for low-income people and people of color who are transgender, intersex, or gender non-conforming.

As you stand in front of the statue of Marsha P. Johnson and Sylvia Rivera, take a moment to reflect on their incredible contributions to the LGBTQ+ community. Their bravery, resilience, and unwavering dedication to equality and justice continue to inspire and guide the fight for LGBTQ+ rights. They will forever be remembered as key figures in the movement, whose impact and legacy will resonate with generations to come.

The creation of the gay pride flag by Gilbert Baker in San Francisco and its evolution to include the trans flag by Daniel Quasar.

As you walk down the vibrant streets of San Francisco, you can't help but notice the brightly colored flags waving proudly in the wind. Among them, the iconic rainbow flag stands tall, often commanding the attention of passersby. But do you know the story behind its creation and evolution?

It all started in 1978, when a young artist named Gilbert Baker was commissioned by Harvey Milk, the first openly gay politician in California, to create a symbol that would represent the LGBTQ+ community. At that time, the only available symbol was the pink triangle, which was used by the Nazis to identify and persecute homosexuals. Baker wanted to create something that would represent hope and pride, rather than oppression.

After weeks of experimentation and collaboration with a team of volunteers, Baker came up with the first version of the gay pride flag. It featured eight stripes of different colors: pink, red, orange, yellow, green, turquoise, indigo, and violet. Each color held a specific meaning – pink for sexuality, red for life, orange for healing, yellow for sunlight, green for nature, turquoise for magic, indigo for serenity, and violet for spirit.

On June 25, 1978, the first-ever pride parade was held in San Francisco, where Baker's hand-sewn flag was carried proudly by thousands of marchers. It became an instant hit and soon spread to other cities, becoming a symbol of the LGBTQ+ community worldwide. However, as the movement grew and progressed, the flag underwent a few changes.

In 1979, the pink and turquoise stripes were removed due to the unavailability of pink fabric and the limited visibility of turquoise. This left seven stripes, which continued to represent the core values of the community. Over the years, the colors have been simplified to six – red, orange, yellow, green, blue, and purple – with different meanings attributed to them.

In 1994, Gilbert Baker created a rainbow flag that measured one mile long and was carried proudly in the 25th anniversary of the Stonewall riots in New York City. This event brought the flag into the mainstream and solidified its position as the universal symbol of pride and acceptance.

However, as the LGBTQ+ community continued to fight for inclusivity, another flag was created to represent the transgender community in 1999. Designed by Monica Helms, the trans flag features five stripes – light blue, pink, white, light pink, and light blue – representing transgender individuals' journey from male to female and vice versa. This flag acknowledges and celebrates the diversity within the LGBTQ+ community, highlighting the inclusivity and intersectionality of the movement.

In 2018, on the 40th anniversary of the gay pride flag, Daniel Quasar, a designer and activist, created the 'progress flag,' a version of the flag that incorporated the trans flag and a chevron representing marginalized communities, such as people of color and those living with HIV. This new flag represented the continued fight for equality and the need to recognize and uplift all individuals within the community.

Today, the Rainbow Pride flag and the Trans Pride flag continue to be powerful symbols of love, acceptance, and equality. They remind us of the progress that has been made and the continuous journey towards a more inclusive and compassionate society. It is a reminder that love knows no boundaries, and every individual deserves to be celebrated for who they are. As you look at the flags flying high, let them be a reminder of the powerful and diverse community that stands together and continues to march towards a brighter and more accepting future.

The role of the leather community in the LGBTQ+ movement

From the colorful flags fluttering at Pride parades to the powerful speeches given at LGBTQ+ rallies, the community has been making strides in the fight for equality and acceptance. However, there is a lesser-known group within the community that has played a significant role in shaping the movement - the leather community.

The leather community is a subculture within the broader LGBTQ+ community that is often misunderstood and misrepresented. They are often associated with sexual fetishes and kinks, but in reality, their role in the LGBTQ+ movement goes far beyond the bedroom.

The leather community emerged in the 1950s and 1960s as a way for gay men to embrace their sexuality and masculinity in a society that deemed it immoral. It was a way to push back against the rigid gender norms and expectations placed upon them and create a space where they could be themselves without fear of discrimination.

One of the most significant ways that the leather community has contributed to the LGBTQ+ movement is through their activism. They were one of the first groups to organize protests and demonstrations for LGBTQ+ rights. In 1965, the first organized LGBT civil rights demonstrations took place in Philadelphia and Washington, D.C., organized by the leather community. These early protests paved the way for the larger, more visible LGBTQ+ rights movements that followed.

The leather community also played a crucial role in the fight against HIV/AIDS. During the height of the epidemic in the 1980s and 1990s, when there was little understanding and support for those affected, the leather community stepped up to take care of their own. They created organizations, such as the Leather Archives & Museum and The Leather Journal, to provide education, resources, and support to those within the community.

Moreover, the leather community has been a strong advocate for sexual freedom and expression. They challenged the idea that one's sexuality was something to be ashamed of and instead embraced it as a source of pride and power. This celebration of sexual diversity and openness has been crucial in breaking down societal stigmas and creating a more inclusive environment for the LGBTQ+ community.

But perhaps the most significant contribution of the leather community to the LGBTQ+ movement is the concept of consent. Through their emphasis on consent and communication, the leather community has helped shape the conversation around sexual assault and consent within the LGBTQ+ community and beyond. They have shown that consent is not only necessary but can also be empowering, leading to a more respectful and safe community for all.

In conclusion, the leather community continues to play a vital role in the LGBTQ+ movement. They have fought for rights and equality, stood up for their community during times of crisis, and championed sexual freedom and consent. While they may not always be in the spotlight, their contributions are invaluable and have helped pave the way towards a more inclusive and accepting society for all. Their unwavering commitment to their community and their values make them an essential and enduring part of the LGBTQ+ movement.

The Handkerchief Code and its significance in LGBTQ+ history

You are standing outside a bustling gay bar in the 1970s, anxiously scanning the crowd for any signs of acceptance. It wasn't always safe to be open about your sexuality, and identifying with others in the LGBTQ+ community could be risky. That's where the handkerchief code comes in – a nonverbal way to communicate your identity and desires safely. Let's take a closer look at this fascinating part of LGBTQ+ history and its significance.

The handkerchief code, also known as the hanky code, was a discreet way for LGBTQ+ individuals to communicate their sexual preferences and identities, primarily within the leather and BDSM communities. It involved wearing a colored handkerchief in your back pocket, with each color and placement symbolizing a different preference. For example, a yellow handkerchief on the left meant you were interested in "water sports" (urine play), while a light blue handkerchief on the right meant you were looking for a "top" or dominant partner.

The code originated in the 1970s during the rise of gay bars and clubs in major cities, where homosexuality was still heavily stigmatized and criminalized. It provided a way for people to safely connect and explore their sexuality without the fear of judgment or persecution.

The significance of the handkerchief code goes beyond its practical use as a communication tool. It represented a sense of unity and pride within the LGBTQ+ community, many of whom were afraid to be open about their identities. By wearing these handkerchiefs, individuals were announcing their presence and celebrating their sexual desires, often in the face of societal norms and expectations.

The code also allowed for a sense of individuality and diversity within the community. With each color representing a different identity and preference, it showed that there was no one way to be LGBTQ+. It celebrated the uniqueness and complexity of each person's sexuality and desires.

The handkerchief code also had a significant impact on the development of the LGBTQ+ community. It created a sense of belonging and camaraderie, especially for those who may have otherwise felt isolated and alone. It paved the way for more open communication and acceptance within the community, as people were able to connect and explore their identities freely.

As time went on, the handkerchief code evolved and became more mainstream, spreading beyond just the leather and BDSM communities. Today, it is seen as a symbol of solidarity and pride within the LGBTQ+ community, with people wearing handkerchiefs in pride parades and other events as a nod to their history and culture.

In summary , the handkerchief code may seem like a simple and subtle way to communicate, but its significance in LGBTQ+ history is immeasurable. It provided a safe way for people to explore and express their sexuality, while also creating a sense of unity and diversity within the community. As we continue to strive for acceptance and equality, let's not forget the importance of our past and the handkerchief code's role in shaping the present.

Chapter 2

Understanding LGBTQ+ Identities

Imagine that you are walking down a busy street, filled with colorful flags, vibrant outfits, and energetic music. As you take in the sights and sounds, you notice a group of individuals holding hands and smiling at each other. They come in all shapes, sizes, and genders, and you can't help but feel drawn to their diverse and inclusive energy. You may wonder, who are they? What do those flags represent? What is it like to be a part of this community?

The group of people you encountered are part of the LGBTQ+ community, which stands for lesbian, gay, bisexual, transgender, queer/questioning, and other sexual and gender identities. This community encompasses a wide range of people who identify as anything other than heterosexual and cisgender (identifying with the gender they were assigned at birth). But being a part of this community goes beyond just labels; it's about understanding the unique experiences, struggles, and identities that make up the LGBTQ+ community.

First, let's break down the acronym. Lesbian refers to women who are attracted to other women, while gay is often used to describe men who are attracted to other men. Bisexual individuals are attracted to people regardless of their gender, while transgender individuals have a gender identity that differs from the sex they were assigned at birth. Queer is an umbrella term that can be used to describe anyone who identifies as anything other than heterosexual or cisgender. It's important to note that these terms are constantly evolving, and someone's identity may not fit neatly into one specific label.

Next, let's dive deeper into the diverse identities that make up the LGBTQ+ community. Pansexual individuals are attracted to people regardless of their gender identity, while asexual individuals do not experience sexual attraction. Non-binary individuals identify as a gender that is not exclusively male or female, and genderqueer individuals see themselves as both or neither. These are just a few examples, but there are countless other identities that exist within the LGBTQ+ community and each one is unique and valid.

But why is it important to understand these identities? For starters, it's essential to recognize and respect the diversity within the LGBTQ+ community. By acknowledging and educating ourselves about the different identities, we can better understand and support our friends, family members, or community members who may identify as LGBTQ+.

It's also crucial to understand the struggles and challenges that individuals within the LGBTQ+ community may face. Discrimination, hate crimes, and lack of legal protections are just some of the issues that LGBTQ+ individuals may encounter. Even within the community, certain identities may face discrimination, such as transgender individuals or people of color who identify as LGBTQ+. By understanding these struggles, we can work towards creating a more inclusive and accepting society for everyone.

Moreover, understanding LGBTQ+ identities means acknowledging the beauty and strength of this community. Despite facing discrimination and adversity, the LGBTQ+ community continues to thrive and celebrate their identities. By embracing diversity and inclusivity, we can create a world where everyone is free to express their true selves without fear of judgment or discrimination.

In conclusion, understanding LGBTQ+ identities goes beyond just knowing the acronym. It means recognizing and respecting the diverse range of sexual and gender identities that exist and understanding the struggles and injustices that members of this community may face. But it also means celebrating the strength, resilience, and beauty of this community, and working towards a more inclusive and accepting world for all. So, next time you see a group of LGBTQ+ individuals, you'll know that they are more than just a label, they are a community filled with love, acceptance, and diversity.

Exploring sexual orientations beyond homosexuality, including asexuality, pansexuality, and demisexuality.

You may have heard about various sexual orientations beyond the commonly known homosexual and heterosexual identities. Many people tend to think that there are only two options when it comes to sexual orientation - you are either attracted to the same gender or opposite gender. But the truth is, human sexuality is not so black and white. In fact, there are many other sexual identities that exist and are gaining more recognition and understanding in our society today.

One of these sexual orientations is asexuality. Simply put, asexuality refers to a lack of sexual attraction or desire towards anyone, regardless of their gender. This can be a confusing concept for those who have only known sexual desire as a natural and integral part of human behavior. But for those who identify as asexual, it is a valid and very real sexual orientation. Asexuality is not the same as celibacy or abstinence, as it is not a choice to abstain from sexual activities but rather a lack of sexual attraction. Asexual individuals may still engage in romantic relationships or have emotional connections, just without the desire for sexual intimacy.

Another lesser-known sexual orientation is pansexuality, which is often confused with bisexuality. Pansexuality refers to an individual who is attracted to people regardless of their gender identity or sexual orientation. Bisexuality is often seen as being attracted to both men and women, but pansexuality goes beyond the gender binary and includes attraction to non-binary and gender fluid individuals. Pansexuality recognizes that gender identity is not a defining factor in one's attraction towards another person.

Demisexual is yet another term that is gaining recognition. Demisexuality refers to an individual who only experiences sexual attraction towards someone after a strong emotional connection has been established. This is different from asexuality as demisexual individuals do experience attraction but only in certain circumstances. For example, a demisexual person may only feel attracted to someone they have known for a long time and have developed an emotional bond with, as opposed to immediate sexual attraction based solely on appearance.

It is crucial to understand that sexual orientation is a spectrum, and each individual's experience is unique and valid. Exploring and recognizing these different sexual orientations beyond the traditional heterosexual and homosexual identities is essential, as it helps to break down stereotypes and stigmas and promotes a more inclusive and understanding society.

However, it is also important to note that these sexual orientations are not a trend or a choice. They are innate and part of one's identity. It is not appropriate to invalidate or discredit someone's sexual orientation because it may not fit into the societal norms. Acceptance and understanding are crucial in creating a safe and inclusive environment for all individuals, regardless of their sexual orientation.

It is essential to explore and understand sexual orientations beyond the traditional binary identities. Asexuality, pansexuality, and demisexuality are just a few examples of the diverse spectrum of human sexuality. Each person's identity is unique and valid, and it is crucial to promote inclusivity and acceptance of all sexual orientations. By recognizing and understanding these different sexual orientations, we can break down barriers and create a more inclusive and understanding society for all.

Discussion on romantic orientations and their importance, particularly for asexual individuals.

As a person who identifies as asexual or on the asexual spectrum, you may have come across the term 'romantic orientation' in your journey of self-discovery. While sexual orientation refers to who you are sexually attracted to, romantic orientation is about who you are romantically attracted to. In simple terms, it is the type of emotional and/or romantic connection that you are drawn to.

For most people, their romantic and sexual orientations align and they are attracted to both the same gender and the opposite gender. However, for asexual individuals, their romantic orientation may not always align with their sexual orientation, making it a much more complex concept.

There are many different romantic orientations,

and it is crucial to understand and discuss them to better understand yourself and your place in the world. Let's explore some of the most common romantic orientations and their importance, particularly for asexual individuals.

1. Heteroromantic

Heteroromantic individuals are those who experience romantic attraction towards people of the opposite gender. This is the most widely recognized and accepted romantic orientation in society, and thus, heteroromantic individuals often face less discrimination and social stigma.

2. Homoromantic

Similar to heteroromantic, homoromantic individuals experience romantic attraction towards people of the same gender. As society becomes more accepting of different sexual orientations, homoromantic individuals are finding more visibility and acceptance.

3. Biromantic

Biromantic individuals are romantically

attracted to both males and females. This may align with a person's bisexual identity, or they may only experience romantic attraction towards both genders while still being on the asexual spectrum.

4. Aromantic

Aromantic individuals do not experience romantic attraction towards anyone. This is not to say that they do not experience love or form close bonds with others, but they do not have a desire for romantic relationships.

5. Demiromantic

Demiromantic individuals are on the asexual spectrum and experience romantic attraction only after developing a strong emotional connection with someone. This is different from demisexual, which refers to someone who only experiences sexual attraction after forming a strong emotional bond.

Now that we have talked about some of the different romantic orientations, let's discuss why it is essential for asexual individuals to understand and identify with their romantic orientation.

Firstly, understanding your romantic orientation can help you navigate your relationships better. A romantic relationship can be challenging to maintain when there are differences in levels of attraction and desire for intimacy. Knowing your romantic orientation can help you communicate your needs and boundaries with your partner and create a relationship that works for both of you.

Furthermore, identifying with a specific romantic orientation can bring a sense of validation and belonging. Asexuality is still not well understood or recognized by society, and many asexual individuals struggle with feeling like they do not fit in or that there is something wrong with them. By identifying with a romantic orientation, they can find a sense of community and connection with others who share similar experiences.

Moreover, understanding your romantic orientation can alleviate internalized pressures and expectations. In a society that often equates love with sex, asexual individuals can feel pressured to engage in romantic relationships that do not align with their desires. Recognizing and embracing their romantic orientation can help them embrace and celebrate their asexuality, without feeling the need to conform to societal expectations.

The discussion on romantic orientations is crucial for asexual individuals as it can help them better understand themselves, navigate their relationships, and find a sense of community and acceptance. Whether you identify as heteroromantic, aromantic, or any other romantic orientation, it is a significant and valid part of who you are. Embrace and own your romantic orientation, and know that there is a place for you in the diverse world of relationships and love.

Inclusivity of nonbinary and genderqueer identities, as well as the experiences of gender non-conforming individuals.

As you walk down the street, you pass by people of all shapes and sizes, races, and cultures. Some may be dressed in jeans and t-shirts, others in fancy dresses or suits. But have you ever stopped to think about the complex and diverse identities that lie beneath the surface? In today's society, we are slowly moving towards a more inclusive and accepting world, but there is still so much work to be done when it comes to understanding and embracing nonbinary and genderqueer identities.

First, let's define these terms. Nonbinary refers to people who do not identify as either male or female, and genderqueer is an umbrella term for individuals who do not conform to traditional gender norms. This includes people who identify as agender (having no gender), genderfluid (fluctuating between different genders), or third gender.

Imagine living in a world where you are constantly told that there are only two options for gender - male or female. Everything from bathroom signs to clothing stores is divided into these two categories, and if you don't fit into either one, you feel like an outsider. This is the reality for many nonbinary and genderqueer individuals.

Growing up, you may have been taught that there are strict rules and expectations for how boys and girls should behave, dress, and express themselves. As a result, many people who do not conform to these societal norms may experience discrimination, bullying, and even violence. This can lead to feelings of shame, confusion, and isolation.

For gender non-conforming individuals, everyday tasks can become a source of anxiety. Something as simple as filling out a form that requires you to choose 'male' or 'female' can be a daunting task. You may also face challenges when it comes to accessing healthcare and receiving proper support and understanding from medical professionals. This lack of inclusion and understanding can have serious consequences for the mental and physical well-being of gender non-conforming individuals.

But despite these challenges, the nonbinary and genderqueer community continues to push for inclusivity and visibility. They are fighting for gender neutral options on official documents, gender-free bathrooms, and acceptance in all areas of society.

For those who identify as nonbinary or genderqueer, finding a community of like-minded individuals can be a crucial source of support. Whether it's through online forums, local support groups, or attending pride events, these spaces allow individuals to connect with others who understand and accept them for who they are.

It's important for all of us to educate ourselves about these identities and be allies to the nonbinary and genderqueer community. This can mean using gender-neutral language, asking for someone's preferred pronouns, and standing up against discrimination and stigma.

Inclusivity of nonbinary and genderqueer identities is not a trend or a political statement - it is a fundamental human right. Everyone deserves to be seen, heard, and respected for who they are, regardless of their gender identity. So the next time you come across someone who identifies as nonbinary or genderqueer, remember to be open-minded and understanding. Because in a world where gender is not limited to just two boxes, we should all strive to be more inclusive and accepting.

Different types of sexual orientations within the LGBTQIA2S+ spectrum

When it comes to sexual orientation, many people often assume that there are only two options: being straight or being gay. However, the reality is much more diverse and complex. The LGBTQIA2S+ spectrum includes a wide range of sexual orientations, each with their own unique experiences and challenges and also LGBTQIA2S stands for Lesbian, Gay, Bisexual, Transgender, Queer/Questioning, Intersex, Asexual, Two spirit. So let's look deeper and explore the different types of sexual orientations within this spectrum.

First and foremost, it's important to understand that sexual orientation refers to an individual's emotional, romantic, and/or sexual attraction to others. It is not the same as gender identity, which is a person's internal sense of their own gender. And within the LGBTQIA2S+ spectrum, there are numerous sexual orientations that fall under the umbrella term of non-heterosexual.

Starting with the most well-known, there is homosexuality, also known as being gay or lesbian. This refers to individuals who are attracted to people of the same gender or sex. For example, a woman who is exclusively attracted to other women would identify as a lesbian.

On the other hand, there is heterosexuality, which refers to those who are attracted to people of the opposite gender or sex. This is what society often considers the norm and is also known as being straight.

Moving on to bisexuality, sometimes referred to as being bi, this is when someone is attracted to two or more genders. It's important to note that being bisexual doesn't necessarily mean you are equally attracted to all genders - some may have a preference towards one or more genders over the others.

Pansexuality is a term that has been gaining

more recognition and refers to individuals who are attracted to people of all genders. The 'pan' prefix comes from the Greek word for 'all,' indicating that this sexual orientation transcends gender.

Then there is asexual, which refers to individuals who do not experience sexual attraction towards any gender. It's important to note that being asexual does not mean someone is incapable of love or forming emotional connections with others. It simply means that they do not experience sexual desire.

Some may also identify as demisexual, which falls under the asexual spectrum. This refers to individuals who only experience sexual attraction after developing a strong emotional bond with someone.

Other sexual orientations that are not as commonly known or acknowledged include polysexuality, which is the attraction to multiple genders, and graysexuality, which falls between being asexual and sexual.

Within the LGBTQIA2S+ spectrum, there are also differing experiences for individuals who are transgender or non-binary. Their gender identity may not align with the gender assigned to them at birth and can have a significant impact on their sexual orientation. For example, someone who is assigned female at birth but identifies as a man may identify as a homosexual when attracted to other men.

Lastly, it's important to note that sexual orientation is not limited to these identities and experiences and is constantly evolving as society and individuals expand their understanding and language for self-expression.

In conclusion, the LGBTQIA2S+ spectrum encompasses a wide range of sexual orientations that go beyond the traditional heteronormative view. Each identity and experience within this spectrum is valid and deserving of recognition, acceptance, and respect. By educating ourselves on these differences, we can foster a more inclusive and understanding society for all.

Chapter 3

Navigating Modern LGBTQ+ Issues

You wake up on a sunny Saturday morning, excited for the day ahead. You and your partner have plans to attend a Pride parade in your city, celebrating the vibrant and diverse LGBTQ+ community. As you put on your rainbow-colored outfit, you can't help but reflect on the progress and challenges faced by the community in recent years.

The modern LGBTQ+ community has come a long way since the Stonewall Riots of 1969, which marked a turning point in the fight for equal rights. While there have been significant improvements in terms of legal rights and societal acceptance, navigating the complex landscape of modern LGBTQ+ issues can still be overwhelming and confusing.

One of the most pressing issues faced by the community today is the constant battle against discrimination. Despite the legalization of same-sex marriage in many countries, there are still instances of workplace discrimination, hate crimes, and bullying based on sexual orientation and gender identity. It can be exhausting constantly having to defend your love and right to exist in a world that continues to question your very existence.

Another issue that often goes unnoticed is the lack of representation in mainstream media. For years, the LGBTQ+ community has been portrayed as villains or comedic relief, reducing their identities to mere stereotypes. It's frustrating to see your identity reduced to a punchline or only represented in a negative light. However, with the rise of social media and marginalized voices being amplified, the community is finally starting to see more authentic and diverse representation.

As you and your partner arrive at the parade, you feel a sense of freedom and belonging, surrounded by a sea of rainbow flags and smiling faces. It's a stark contrast to the world outside, where you constantly have to be on guard and hide your true self. However, it's not all rainbows and butterflies. There is still a lot of work to be done within the community itself.

While the acronym LGBTQ+ includes a range of identities, the reality is that not all members of the community are accepted equally. Transgender individuals, especially, face high levels of discrimination and violence, even within the LGBTQ+ community. It's disheartening to see that the community, which is supposed to be a safe haven, can also be a source of exclusion and discrimination.

Another issue that often divides the community is the ongoing debate about whether or not to assimilate into mainstream society. On one hand, assimilation can lead to greater acceptance and rights, but on the other hand, it can also erase the unique identities and experiences of the community. It's a complex issue that continues to be a topic of discussion within the community.

As the parade begins and you march alongside your fellow community members, you feel a sense of unity and resilience. You see the younger generation marching proudly, and you can't help but feel hopeful for the future. They are growing up in a world that is more accepting and inclusive, but it's important to continue fighting for their rights and for the rights of all members of the community.

As the parade comes to an end, you and your partner hold hands and take in the beautiful chaos and love around you. Despite the challenges and issues faced by the modern LGBTQ+ community, there is a sense of hope and acceptance, and that is worth celebrating. Navigating modern LGBTQ+ issues may not be easy, but with the support of each other and allies, we will continue to make strides towards equality and create a more inclusive world for all.

The influence of social media on queer youth and its associated challenges.

You are a young queer person navigating the ever-changing landscape of social media. As you scroll through your newsfeed, you see an influx of rainbow flags, #PrideMonth posts, and images of happy, confident queer individuals. It's a reassuring feeling to see your community being celebrated and represented, but behind the uplifting façade lies a less talked about reality - the influence of social media on queer youth and the challenges that come along with it.

On the surface, social media seems like a safe space for queer individuals, a platform to connect with like-minded people and express their identities freely. But the truth is, social media has its own set of challenges and struggles for queer youth. The pressure to curate a perfect online persona, the fear of being outed, and the constant comparison to others' seemingly perfect lives can take a toll on a queer person's mental health.

One of the most prominent influences of social media on queer youth is the pressure to fit into societal norms and expectations. Being queer in a heteronormative society, it's no surprise that queer youth often feel the need to conform to mainstream beauty standards and societal norms in order to be accepted and validated. This can lead to a constant sense of insecurity, self-doubt, and even body dysmorphia in some cases. Platforms like Instagram and Snapchat, with their emphasis on flawless filters and carefully curated feeds, can exacerbate these feelings, making young queer individuals feel like they don't belong in their own community.

Another significant challenge that comes with social media is the fear of being outed. For many young queer individuals, social media is their main source of support and connection within the community. However, with the rise of cyberbullying and online harassment, there is a legitimate fear of being outed to unsupportive family members, friends or acquaintances. This fear can lead to the use of fake accounts or self-censorship, taking away a person's ability to authentically express themselves online.

Moreover, social media can also create a false sense of community for queer youth. While it is a great platform to connect with people who share similar identities and experiences, it can also lead to a lack of real-life connections. This can be especially harmful for those who may not have a supportive community offline. The constant online validation and curated interactions can feel isolating and make it difficult for a young queer person to form meaningful, in-person relationships.

In addition to these challenges, social media can also perpetuate stereotypes and discrimination against queer individuals. With the viral spread of memes, jokes, and hate speech, harmful stereotypes about the queer community are constantly reinforced. This can negatively impact a young person's self-esteem and lead to feelings of shame and self-hatred.

But it's not all doom and gloom. Despite its challenges, social media has also played a crucial role in amplifying queer voices, creating a sense of solidarity and promoting acceptance and understanding. The internet has provided an open platform for the LGBTQ+ community to share their stories, educate others, and advocate for their rights. It has also allowed young queer individuals to explore and express their identities in a safe and inclusive space.

As a queer youth, it's important to recognize the influence of social media on your mental health and be mindful of the impact it can have on your self-esteem and sense of belonging. Surrounding yourself with supportive and understanding online communities, limiting your social media usage, and prioritizing your mental well-being can help navigate through the challenges of social media.

The influence of social media on queer youth and its associated challenges cannot be ignored.

As we continue to navigate the digital world, it's important to create a safe and inclusive online space for young queer individuals to thrive and express themselves authentically. Let's use the power of social media to uplift and celebrate our community, rather than perpetuating harmful stereotypes and pressures. You are not alone in this digital journey, and by being aware, you can challenge the negative influences and create a more positive and empowering virtual world for yourself and others.

Suggestions for meeting other LGBTQ+ youth in safe environments.

As a member of the LGBTQ+ community, you may often feel like you are the only one going through certain experiences and struggles. However, you are not alone. There are many other youth out there just like you, looking for a safe and accepting environment to express their true selves. Here are some suggestions for meeting other LGBTQ+ youth in safe environments:

1. Join local LGBTQ+ organizations and clubs: Look for LGBTQ+ organizations and clubs in your city or town. These groups provide a safe space for LGBTQ+ youth to gather, share their stories, and support each other. They also organize various activities and events, such as movie nights, game nights, and pride parades, where you can meet other LGBTQ+ youth.

2. Attend LGBTQ+ youth conferences or retreats: Conferences and retreats specifically for LGBTQ+ youth are great opportunities to meet others who share similar experiences and interests. These events often include workshops, discussions, and social gatherings where you can connect with other like-minded individuals.

3. Utilize social media: Social media platforms, such as Instagram, Twitter, and Tumblr, have vibrant LGBTQ+ communities where you can connect with other youth from all over the world. Follow hashtags like #LGBTQYouth, #GayTeen, or #TransYouth to find and interact

with others who are also looking for safe and inclusive spaces.

4. Join online support groups: There are many online support groups and forums dedicated to LGBTQ+ youth, where you can share your experiences, seek advice, and find support from others who understand what you are going through. These groups provide a safe and convenient way to connect with other LGBTQ+ youth, especially if you live in a place where it may not be safe to be openly LGBTQ+.

5. Volunteer for LGBTQ+ organizations: Volunteering for organizations that support the LGBTQ+ community is a great way to meet other like-minded individuals while making a positive impact. You can find opportunities to volunteer at pride events, LGBTQ+ youth centers, and other organizations that work towards promoting equality and inclusivity.

6. Attend LGBTQ+ friendly events and activities: Keep an eye out for LGBTQ+ friendly

events and activities in your community, such as pride festivals, concerts, art shows, and book clubs. These events often attract a diverse range of people, including LGBTQ+ youth, and provide a welcoming and safe environment to connect and have fun.

7. Reach out to LGBTQ+ youth online: If you are struggling to find LGBTQ+ youth in your local community, consider connecting with others online. You can join forums, groups, and social media pages specifically for LGBTQ+ youth. Building connections online can lead to meaningful friendships and support networks.

Remember to always prioritize your safety when meeting new people, especially as a member of the LGBTQ+ community. Meet in public places, let someone know where you are going and who you are meeting, and trust your instincts. With these suggestions in mind, you can feel more confident in finding and connecting with other LGBTQ+ youth in safe and welcoming environments. So step out and take a chance, you never know who you might meet and how they could positively impact your life.

Extensive information on safe sex practices, including guidance on navigating digital spaces and avoiding predators.

You wake up every morning and look in the mirror, wondering if today is the day you finally have the confidence to be yourself. You scroll through social media, seeing all the perfect lives and bodies plastered across your screen, and you can't help but feel a twinge of envy. How can you ever measure up to what society deems "normal"?

As a member of the LGBTQ+ community, you face these struggles every day. From navigating the world of dating to simply being comfortable in your own skin, it can feel overwhelming and isolating. But I'm here to tell you that you are not alone. Your identity is something to be proud of, and it's time to conquer the confidence to fully embrace it.

First and foremost, understanding your own body and pleasure is essential. As a member of the LGBTQ+ community, you may have unique needs and desires that require careful attention and exploration. This means taking the time to understand your own anatomy, as well as being vocal and clear about what you do and do not want.

It's also crucial to have open and honest conversations with your partner(s) about sexual history and STI testing. This includes discussing any potential risks or health concerns before engaging in any sexual activity. Remember, there is no such thing as too much communication when it comes to protecting your health.

In today's digital age, it's becoming increasingly common to meet potential partners through dating and hookup apps. While these platforms can be a great way to connect with others, they also come with their own set of risks. It's important to be aware of online predators and scammers who may attempt to exploit vulnerable individuals. Always trust your gut instincts and never be afraid to block or report anyone who makes you feel uncomfortable.

Another thing to keep in mind is the importance of practicing safe sex, regardless of sexual orientation or gender identity. This includes using protection, such as condoms, dental dams, and gloves, to reduce the risk of STIs. It's also important to be mindful of substances that may impair judgment and increase the likelihood of engaging in risky behaviors.

Furthermore, navigating consent is essential in any sexual encounter. Remember, the absence of a clear "no" does not equate to a "yes". Consent should be enthusiastic, ongoing, and freely given by all parties involved. If you or your partner(s) are under the influence of substances, consent cannot be given.

In addition to traditional safe sex practices, the digital world also brings the need for protecting your online identity and privacy. This means being cautious of giving out personal information and photos that could potentially be used against you. If you're unsure about a potential partner's intentions, take the time to get to know them before divulging any personal information or meeting in person.

Above all else, know that your identity is valid and deserving of love and respect. No one should ever make you feel ashamed or lesser because of who you are. By understanding and practicing safe sex, both physically and digitally, you are taking the necessary steps to protect yourself and your community.

Support for individuals in abusive relationships and guidance for dealing with school and friends.

You have always known deep down that you were different. Growing up, you didn't quite fit in with the other kids. You were more interested in dolls than cars, in playing dress-up than sports. But you didn't understand why you felt this way, why you didn't fit into the societal norms of what a boy or a girl should be. It wasn't until you discovered the LGBTQ+ community that everything started to make sense.

But along with this discovery came fear. Fear of not being accepted, fear of judgment, fear of losing the people in your life. You found yourself in a constant state of anxiety, constantly questioning whether it was okay to be who you were.

And then you met them. The person who made you feel seen, understood, and loved for exactly who you are. You thought you had found your happily ever after, but instead, you found yourself in an abusive relationship.

It started with small things, like controlling what you wore or who you talked to. But as time went on, it escalated to physical and emotional abuse. You felt trapped, scared, and alone. You didn't know who you could turn to or if anyone would believe you.

But the truth is, you are not alone. LGBTQ+ individuals are at a higher risk of experiencing abuse in relationships due to the stigma and discrimination they face. But there is support available for you.

The first step is to reach out. It can be scary, but there are resources available for LGBTQ+ individuals experiencing abuse. The Trevor Project, for example, offers a 24/7 crisis hotline specifically for LGBTQ+ youth. They also have online chat and text options if you are not comfortable speaking on the phone.

Additionally, The National Domestic Violence Hotline has resources for LGBTQ+ individuals, including a chat option, and can help you create a safety plan.

You may also feel like you have no one to turn to at school or among your friends. But there are supportive communities and organizations out there. Look for LGBTQ+ support groups in your area or on social media. These spaces can be a source of comfort, understanding, and guidance for navigating your identity and dealing with the challenges you may face.

It's important to remember that you deserve to be treated with respect and love, and that includes within your relationships. No one has the right to control, manipulate, or abuse you. You may also feel pressure to stay in the relationship because of your identity, but remember that being part of the LGBTQ+ community does not mean accepting abuse. You deserve to be with someone who loves and respects you for who you are.

Unfortunately, dealing with abuse can sometimes mean losing friends or feeling like you have to hide your true self. But remember, those who truly care about you will support and stand by you, no matter what. If someone cannot accept and respect your identity, they are not a true friend.

It may also be helpful to seek therapy to process your experiences and learn healthy ways to cope and rebuild your self-confidence. A therapist can also help you navigate coming out, if and when you feel ready, to others who may not be supportive or accepting.

Just because you are struggling now does not mean you will not overcome this and find happiness. You deserve to live a life free from abuse and surrounded by people who love and support you for who you are. Know that you are not alone, and there is a whole community out there ready to welcome you with open arms. Be proud of who you are, and never let anyone make you feel otherwise. Stay strong, and know that you are worthy of joy and love, always.

Recommendations for handling sexual peer pressure and maintaining healthy relationships.

As a member of the LGBTQ+ community, you understand the importance of staying true to yourself and your identity. However, in today's world, there is still a lot of stigma and pressure surrounding sexuality. This can often lead to peer pressure and unhealthy relationships. As you navigate through your journey of self-discovery, it is crucial to have a strong sense of self and the confidence to stand up for yourself. Here are some recommendations for handling sexual peer pressure and maintaining healthy relationships.

First and foremost, it is essential to know your boundaries and communicate them clearly. Peer pressure can come in many forms, and it is common for others to try to push your boundaries. Whether it's through coercion or manipulation, it is crucial to know when to say no and stand your ground. You have the right to decide what you are comfortable with, and it is not your responsibility to please others. Be firm and assertive in communicating your boundaries, and don't be afraid to walk away from any situation that makes you uncomfortable.

In today's society, there is a lot of pressure to conform to certain labels and stereotypes. However, it is crucial to remember that you are not defined by any label. You are a unique individual with your own identity, and you should never feel pressured to fit into a certain mold. It is okay to explore and embrace your sexuality without feeling the need to label yourself. Don't let others dictate how you should identify, and always stay true to yourself and your feelings.

When it comes to relationships, it is vital to establish a healthy and respectful dynamic. This means having open and honest communication, mutual trust and respect, and understanding each other's boundaries. Don't let anyone pressure you into a relationship or try to change who you are to fit into their ideal partner. A healthy relationship is built on acceptance and support, not on trying to change each other.

Maintaining a healthy relationship also means taking care of yourself. It is easy to get caught up in the excitement and passion of a new relationship, but it is crucial to prioritize your mental and emotional well-being. Don't neglect your own needs and wants for the sake of a relationship. Remember to set aside time for yourself, have your own hobbies and interests, and maintain a support system outside of your relationship.

Lastly, always remember that it is okay to seek help and support when needed. It takes courage to speak up and reach out for help, but it is a crucial step in maintaining your mental and emotional well-being. Whether it's talking to a trusted friend or seeking professional counseling, don't be afraid to ask for support. There is no shame in needing help, and it is a sign of strength to acknowledge and address any struggles you may be facing.

With all that , navigating through sexuality and relationships can be challenging, especially in a world obsessed with labels. However, by knowing your boundaries, staying true to yourself, and prioritizing your well-being, you can confidently handle sexual peer pressure and maintain healthy relationships. Remember, you are not defined by anyone else's expectations or judgments, and your happiness and well-being should always be your priority. Stay proud and stay true to yourself always.

Safe sex education for LGBTQ+ individuals

As an LGBTQ+ individual, you may often feel like your identity is constantly being labeled and defined by society. However, in order to truly embrace your authentic self and find joy in your identity, it is important to also prioritize your sexual health and well-being.

First and foremost, it is crucial to understand that safe sex education for LGBTQ+ individuals is not the same as that for heterosexual individuals. The LGBTQ+ community faces unique challenges and risks when it comes to sexual health, and it is important to receive education and resources that are tailored to your specific needs. That's where LGBTQ+ affirming and inclusive sex education comes in.

Rather than focusing solely on traditional forms of contraception and prevention of STIs, LGBTQ+ safe sex education also includes topics such as gender identity, sexual orientation, consent, and communication in relationships. These are all important aspects of sexual health that are often overlooked or neglected in mainstream sex education.

Furthermore, it is important to find a safe and inclusive space where you can receive this education without fear of judgment or discrimination. This can be in the form of LGBTQ+ support groups, community centers, or even online resources. By learning in a supportive and affirming environment, you can feel comfortable expressing your identity and asking any questions you may have.

One key aspect of safe sex education for LGBTQ+ individuals is understanding the various forms of protection and their effectiveness for different types of sexual activities. This can include condoms, dental dams, and lubricants, as well as the use of PrEP for HIV prevention. It is important to remember that even within the LGBTQ+ community, there is diversity in the ways individuals engage in sexual activities, and it is important to always prioritize open and honest communication about boundaries, protection, and consent.

Another important aspect of safe sex education for LGBTQ+ individuals is acknowledging the stigma and discrimination that our community faces in accessing healthcare. Many medical professionals are not trained or educated on LGBTQ+ health, and this can lead to a lack of understanding and even mistreatment. It is crucial to find healthcare providers who are knowledgeable and affirming of your identity, so that you can feel comfortable discussing your sexual health without fear of judgment or discrimination.

In addition to understanding the physical aspects of safe sex, it is also important to address the mental and emotional well-being of LGBTQ+ individuals. The intersections of identity, sexuality, and gender can be complex and can sometimes lead to feelings of shame, guilt, or confusion. Safe sex education should include discussions on these topics and provide resources for mental health support.

Lastly, it is important to remember that safe sex education is an ongoing process. As you continue to grow and evolve, so will your sexual health needs. It is important to stay informed and up-to-date on new methods of protection and healthcare resources that become available.

Thus, safe sex education for LGBTQ+ individuals is essential in empowering us to take control of our sexual health and well-being. By seeking out LGBTQ+ affirming education, finding inclusive healthcare providers, and prioritizing open and honest communication in sexual relationships, we can conquer confidence and find joy in our identities. Remember, your identity is not defined by labels, but by the pride and joy that comes from embracing your authentic self.

Chapter 4

Exploring LGBTQ+ Topics

As you sit down with your morning cup of coffee and scroll through your social media feed, you see an article about the LGBTQ+ community. It catches your attention, but you hesitate to click on it. After all, you don't know much about this topic and are not sure if you will understand it. But something inside of you wants to know more, to understand and explore this often-misunderstood community. You take a deep breath and click on the link, ready to embark on a journey of discovery.

 First things first, what does LGBTQ+ stand for? Well, it is an acronym that represents Lesbian, Gay, Bisexual, Transgender, and Queer/Questioning individuals, with the '+' sign added to be inclusive of other identities. You may have heard these terms before, but do you know what they mean? Let's take a closer look.

Exploring LGBTQ+ topics goes beyond just understanding sexual orientations and gender identities. It involves delving into their histories, cultures, and experiences that have shaped their identities. It is about acknowledging and celebrating their unique perspectives, struggles, and triumphs. It is about breaking down the barriers and boundaries that society has imposed on them and embracing them for who they truly are.

It takes you on a journey through the different intersections of gender, sexuality, race, ethnicity, and class, and how they shape one's sense of self. It brings to the forefront the issues faced by the LGBTQ+ community, such as discrimination, homophobia, and transphobia, and how they have affected individuals' lives.

Let's look into some common misconceptions. One of the biggest myths about the LGBTQ+ community is that being a part of it is a choice. This could not be further from the truth. As mentioned before, one's sexual orientation and gender identity are not a choice, but rather a fundamental part of who they are.

Another misconception is that LGBTQ+ individuals are 'attention-seekers' or are only looking for special rights and privileges. This could not be further from the truth. The reality is that members of the LGBTQ+ community face discrimination and oppression daily, and equality is simply not a reality for them. LGBTQ+ individuals are fighting for basic human rights and acceptance, not for special treatment.

Now, you may be wondering why exploring LGBTQ+ topics is important. Well, for starters, it allows individuals like yourself to gain a better understanding and acceptance of a community that is often marginalized and misunderstood. By educating ourselves, we can become better allies and create a more inclusive and accepting society.

Furthermore, exploring LGBTQ+ topics also allows us to challenge and deconstruct societal norms and stereotypes. It opens the conversation about gender and sexuality, which are often viewed as binary and rigid concepts, and allows for a more nuanced understanding of diversity and inclusivity.

As you continue your exploration of LGBTQ+ topics, keep in mind that everyone's journey is unique and personal. It is not our place to judge or question someone's identity, but rather to listen and learn from their experiences. By being open-minded and supportive, we can create a more understanding and accepting world for everyone.

In conclusion, exploring LGBTQ+ topics is not just about learning new terminology and concepts. It is about empathy, understanding, and creating a more inclusive and accepting world. So the next time you come across an article or a discussion about the LGBTQ+ community, don't hesitate to engage and learn. After all, knowledge is power and change starts with understanding.

Discussion on stereotypes, homophobia, and the process of coming out.

You've lived your whole life feeling different, standing out from the norm. You've always had a nagging feeling that you didn't quite fit in with society's expectations, and you couldn't quite put your finger on why. But as you grew older, and as society's views began to shift, you started to realize that there was a part of you that had been hiding in the shadows, waiting to be heard.

As you started exploring your feelings and identities, you realized that you are part of the LGBTQ+ community. And as you embraced your true self and came out to those around you, you were met with a mix of reactions – some positive and accepting, while others filled with stereotypes and homophobia.

So, let's dive into the discussion on stereotypes, homophobia, and the process of coming out, and explore how they intersect with your journey of self-discovery and conquering confidence.

Stereotypes are harmful and limiting assumptions that society places on individuals based on their gender, sexuality, race, religion, or other aspects of their identities. They are often used to categorize and judge people, boxing them into strict definitions and expectations. And for members of the LGBTQ+ community, stereotypes can be especially damaging.

The media has played a significant role in perpetuating stereotypes about LGBTQ+ individuals, portraying them as flamboyant, promiscuous, and deviant. These harmful representations not only misrepresent the diverse experiences within the community but also contribute to the discrimination and prejudice they face in their daily lives.

Homophobia, or the fear and hatred of homosexuality, is a direct result of these stereotypes and societal expectations. It leads to discrimination, violence, and even laws that deny LGBTQ+ individuals their basic human rights. This fear and hatred are often rooted in ignorance and the misunderstanding of what it means to be part of the LGBTQ+ community.

Growing up in a society that is obsessed with labels can make it difficult for LGBTQ+ individuals to come to terms with their identities. The pressure to fit into a specific box, whether it is heterosexual or LGBTQ+, can be daunting and confusing. And when those labels are filled with negative connotations, it can be even more challenging to embrace and express your true self.

But despite the challenges, you made the brave decision to come out to the world and proudly proclaim who you are. It was a process filled with fear, self-doubt, and vulnerability, but also one of immense strength and courage. As you navigated through this journey, you may have faced rejection, discrimination, and even lost relationships. But you also may have found a sense of freedom and authenticity that you had never experienced before.

Through your journey, you have also discovered the importance of acceptance and support from those around you. You have realized that the labels society places on you do not define you, and it is up to you to define yourself. And in doing so, you have conquered confidence in a world that tries to limit and define you.

As we continue to explore and celebrate LGBTQ+ identities, it is vital to shed light on the harmful effects of stereotypes and homophobia. By breaking down these societal expectations and embracing our true selves, we can create a more inclusive and accepting world for future generations. And by sharing our stories and experiences, we can inspire others to do the same, with confidence and pride.

Addressing sexual health topics, including STIs and safe-sex practices tailored to gender preferences.

As a member of the LGBTQ+ community, exploring your own identity can be both liberating and challenging. While society is making strides towards acceptance and equality, there are still many hurdles to overcome. One of these hurdles is discussing and addressing sexual health. In a world that is obsessed with labels and stereotypes, it can be difficult to have open and honest conversations about sexual health tailored to your gender preferences. However, it is crucial to prioritize your sexual health and stay informed in order to have safe and enjoyable experiences.

First and foremost, it is important to understand that sexual health is not limited to just physical health. It also includes emotional, mental, and social well-being. As an individual who identifies as LGBTQ+, it is necessary to address the unique challenges that we face when it comes to sexual health. Unfortunately, there is a lack of information and resources specifically tailored to our community, making it even more crucial to educate ourselves and have open conversations.

When it comes to sexually transmitted infections (STIs), all individuals, regardless of sexual orientation or gender identity, are at risk. It is a common misconception that same-sex relationships are immune to STIs, but the reality is that any type of sexual activity can transmit infections. It is important to understand the different types of STIs and their symptoms, as well as getting tested regularly. Remember, it is not a reflection of your sexual preferences or identity, it is simply a part of taking care of your health.

It may be uncomfortable, but discussing safe-sex practices is essential for everyone. This includes education on contraceptive methods, consent, and communication. What makes it challenging for members of the LGBTQ+ community is that there is often limited information and resources tailored to our specific needs. For example, discussing safe-sex practices between two men may differ from discussing safe-sex practices between two women. It is important to have open and honest conversations with your sexual partners and to prioritize your safety and well-being.

Another aspect to consider is how some individuals may experience dysphoria or body dysmorphia, which can impact their sexual health and relationships. It is important to prioritize your mental and emotional well-being, as this plays a crucial role in your sexual health as well. Know that it is okay to take time for yourself and focus on your own needs before engaging in sexual activities.

In addition to discussing sexual health, there are also societal pressures that come with being a part of the LGBTQ+ community. Often times, individuals may feel the need to label themselves or conform to societal expectations in order to fit in. However, it is important to remember that your identity is unique and personal to you. Do not let labels dictate your sexual experiences. Embrace your individuality and let go of any expectations or restrictions placed upon you. This is where confidence plays a crucial role.

As you continue to explore your LGBTQ+ identity and navigate the complexities of sexual health, remember to always prioritize yourself and your well-being. Have open and honest conversations with your partners, educate yourself, and practice safe-sex. Let go of labels and expectations, and be confident in who you are. It is only when we conquer our own doubts and insecurities that you can truly revel in the joy and pride of being a part of the LGBTQ+ community.

Exploring LGBTQ+ culture, the dating scene, and the intersection of religion with sexual identity.

When it comes to exploring LGBTQ+ culture, the dating scene and the intersection of religion with sexual identity, there are many aspects and complexities to consider. As a member of this community, you understand firsthand the struggles and triumphs that come with embracing your true self and navigating the world as a queer individual. However, for those who may not be familiar with this community, it can be a bit of a mystery and may require some education and understanding.

First and foremost, it is important to understand that LGBTQ+ culture is not a monolithic entity. It is a vibrant and diverse community made up of individuals with their own unique experiences, identities, and backgrounds. From gay and lesbian to bisexual, transgender, and queer, each letter in the acronym represents a different identity and experience. It is important to recognize and celebrate this diversity, rather than lumping everyone together under one label.

One of the key aspects of LGBTQ+ culture is the dating scene. For many queer individuals, dating can be a challenging and a hard task. From dealing with societal stigma and discrimination to finding potential partners, it is not always easy. However, through the challenges, there is a strong sense of solidarity and support within the community. LGBTQ+ individuals have created their own dating apps, events, and spaces to connect with others who share similar experiences and interests.

When it comes to dating in the LGBTQ+ community, there is also a strong emphasis on consent and open communication. This is often due to the fact that many of them had to navigate relationships and sexual encounters in a world that does not always understand or accept their identities. As a result, there is a heightened awareness and emphasis on creating safe and consensual spaces.

However, one aspect that cannot be ignored when discussing LGBTQ+ dating is the intersection of religion with sexual identity. This can be a difficult and sensitive topic, as the relationship between religion and LGBTQ+ identity is often complicated and varies greatly among individuals. Some individuals may come from religious backgrounds that are accepting and supportive of their identity, while others may have faced rejection and condemnation.

For those who come from more conservative or traditional religious backgrounds, it can be a real struggle to reconcile their faith with their sexual identity. Many fear losing their family, friends, and even their faith community if they come out as LGBTQ+. This brings up questions of acceptance and judgment within their religious communities, and often leads to a sense of isolation and internal conflict.

On the other hand, there are also many religious

individuals who have found acceptance and support within their faith communities. There are churches and religious organizations that are welcoming and affirming of LGBTQ+ identities, providing a sense of belonging and support for those who have often felt rejected by their religious beliefs.

It is important to recognize that the intersection of religion and sexual identity is a complex and personal journey for every individual. As outsiders, it is not our place to judge or impose our own beliefs onto others. Rather, we should strive to create a safe and inclusive space for all, regardless of their religious background or sexual identity.

In the end, exploring LGBTQ+ culture, the dating scene, and the intersection of religion with sexual identity is a journey of self-discovery and acceptance. It requires understanding, empathy, and a willingness to learn from each other. As a member of the LGBTQ+ community, you understand the struggles and triumphs that come with embracing your true self. And as society continues to evolve and become more accepting, it is your responsibility to continue educating and advocating for your community. Let us celebrate our differences and come together in solidarity as we continue to explore and embrace LGBTQ+ culture.

Insights into the experiences of LGBTQ+ individuals beyond sexuality, including activism and building supportive communities.

You are part of the LGBTQ+ community, and you know all too well the struggles and challenges that come with it. From navigating through your own identity, to facing discrimination and bigotry, the journey has not been an easy one. However, beyond your sexuality, there is a whole world of experiences that shape your life as an LGBTQ+ individual.

Activism is a crucial part of the LGBTQ+

community, and it comes in various forms. It can be as simple as participating in Pride events and rallies, or as impactful as speaking up against injustice and advocating for equal rights. Being a part of the LGBTQ+ community means constantly fighting for your rights, and this often involves facing opposition and standing up against prejudices.

The experiences of LGBTQ+ individuals also extend beyond their own personal struggles. Many individuals in the community actively work towards creating a more inclusive and supportive society. From establishing safe spaces and support groups, to organizing workshops and events that promote understanding and acceptance, the LGBTQ+ community has built a strong network of support for those who need it.

One of the key aspects of this community is finding a sense of belonging and creating a support system. For many LGBTQ+ individuals, coming out to their families and friends can be a difficult and challenging experience. This is where the LGBTQ+ community steps in, providing a safe and accepting environment where they can freely express themselves without fear of rejection or discrimination.

This sense of community is also vital for individuals who may not have a supportive family or friends. LGBTQ+ youth who are rejected by their families or forced to leave their homes often find comfort and acceptance within the community. This sense of belonging can be life-saving for those who may otherwise feel isolated and alone in their struggles.

Beyond activism and building supportive communities, the LGBTQ+ community also encompasses a diverse range of experiences. LGBTQ+ individuals come from different backgrounds, cultures, and identities, and their experiences are shaped by various intersecting factors such as race, religion, and socioeconomic status.

Even within the community, individuals may

face different struggles based on their intersecting identities. For example, LGBTQ+ individuals of color may face double discrimination and marginalization due to both their race and sexuality. It is important to acknowledge and understand these differences within the community, and to actively work towards creating an inclusive and intersectional space.

Being a part of the LGBTQ+ community means constantly navigating through a complex web of experiences, challenges, and triumphs. It means finding strength in unity and standing together to fight for equality and acceptance. Beyond your sexuality, you are a multifaceted individual with a unique perspective, and your experiences as an LGBTQ+ person are valid and should be celebrated.

It is about finding your voice, creating a safe and inclusive space, and navigating through the complexities of life as an LGBTQ+ individual. So for anyone who may not fully understand the experiences of the community, take a moment to listen and learn from those who live it every day. And for those who are a part of this community, continue to stand tall and proud, for together, we are stronger.

Chapter 5

Q&A About LGBTQ+ Identity

As you navigate your way through understanding your own identity, you may have questions about what it means to be a part of the LGBTQ+ community. Maybe you've heard the term LGBTQ+ and are curious about what it stands for. Or perhaps you're unsure about your own gender or sexual orientation and want to learn more. Regardless of where you are in your journey, asking questions is an important part of self-discovery and acceptance. So, let's dive into some common questions about LGBTQ+ identity.

Q: What does LGBTQ+ stand for?

A: LGBTQ+ stands for Lesbian, Gay, Bisexual, Transgender, Queer/Questioning, and others. The plus sign at the end represents all other identities within the community such as asexual, pansexual, and non-binary.

Q: What is the difference between gender and sexual orientation?

A: Gender and sexual orientation are two distinct aspects of a person's identity. Gender refers to a person's internal sense of being male, female, or non-binary. Sexual orientation, on the other hand, refers to who a person is attracted to emotionally, romantically, and/or sexually. It is important to note that gender and sexual orientation are not binary and can range on a spectrum.

Q: What does it mean to be transgender?

A: Being transgender means that a person's gender identity does not match the sex they were assigned at birth. This can involve transitioning to live as their true gender, which can include changing their name, pronouns, and possibly undergoing medical procedures like hormone therapy or gender confirmation surgeries.

Q: What does it mean to be queer/questioning?

A: The term queer has historically been used as a derogatory slur but has since been reclaimed by the LGBTQ+ community as an umbrella term for anyone who does not identify as heterosexual or cisgender. Questioning refers to someone who is still exploring their sexual orientation or gender identity and has not yet come to a conclusion or label for themselves.

Q: Can someone be both LGBTQ+ and religious?

A: Absolutely! Being LGBTQ+ and religious are not mutually exclusive. Many religions, including Christianity, Judaism, and Islam, have LGBTQ+ affirming congregations and leaders who embrace and celebrate different sexual orientations and gender identities.

Q: Is being LGBTQ+ a choice?

A: No, being LGBTQ+ is not a choice. Just as a

person does not choose their height or eye color, one does not choose their sexual orientation or gender identity. These aspects of a person's identity are innate and cannot be changed.

Q: Is it okay to ask someone about their gender or sexual orientation?

A: It is not appropriate to ask someone about their gender or sexual orientation unless they have openly shared that information with you. Trust and respect are important factors in a person's choice to disclose their identity, so it's important to let them make that decision for themselves.

Q: What can I do to support the LGBTQ+ community?

A: There are many things you can do to support the LGBTQ+ community. Educate yourself about different identities and issues facing the community, attend pride events, speak out against discrimination and hate, and practice inclusivity and open-mindedness in your daily interactions.

Q: How do I know if I am LGBTQ+?

A: Only you can truly understand your own identity. It is a personal journey and realization that may take time and exploration. If you are questioning your identity, know that it is normal and valid. You can seek support and guidance from trusted friends, family, or organizations such as LGBTQ+ support groups or therapists who specialize in working with this community.

Q: Can a person's sexual orientation or gender identity change over time?

A: Yes, some individuals may experience changes in their sexual orientation or gender identity throughout their lives. For others, their identity may remain consistent. The most important thing is to respect and support individuals regardless of where they are on their journey.

Q: Is being LGBTQ+ a sin?

A: This is a highly debated and personal question that differs based on one's beliefs and values. However, it is essential to recognize that love is not a sin and that individuals should not be judged or discriminated against based on their sexual orientation or gender identity.

Q: What challenges do LGBTQ+ individuals face?

A: Unfortunately, members of the LGBTQ+ community still face discrimination and stigma in many aspects of their lives, including in healthcare, education, employment, and housing. Many also face rejection from family and friends, which can lead to higher rates of mental health issues and homelessness within the community.

It's completely normal to have questions and uncertainties about LGBTQ+ identity, but it's important to remember that everyone's journey is unique. It's also important to remember that the most important thing is to accept yourself and others for who they are. Whether you are a member of the community or an ally, know that you are valid and deserving of love and respect.

Clear explanations of terms such as transvestite, transgender, and transsexual.

As you scroll through your social media feeds, you may have come across terms such as transvestite, transgender, and transsexual. These terms are often used interchangeably, but they actually refer to different aspects of gender identity.

Let's start with transvestite. This term refers to a person who wears clothing that is typically associated with the opposite gender. For example, a man who wears dresses or a woman who wears suits. However, it is important to note that being a transvestite does not necessarily mean that a person identifies as a different gender. It is simply a form of self-expression through clothing.

On the other hand, being transgender means that a person's gender identity does not align with the sex they were assigned at birth. This can mean that a person was assigned male at birth but identifies as a woman, or vice versa. Being transgender is a deeply personal experience, and it is important to respect a person's self-identification.

Now, let's talk about the term transsexual. This is similar to being transgender, but it specifically refers to a person who has undergone medical treatments, such as hormone therapy or gender confirmation surgery, to align their physical body with their gender identity. Transsexual people often face discrimination and prejudice, as their transition challenges societal norms and traditional definitions of gender.

So why do these terms often get mixed up? This can be due to the fact that all of them involve some form of gender identity that may differ from societal norms. However, it is important to understand that each term has its own distinct meaning and should not be used interchangeably.

It is also worth noting that not all transgender or transsexual individuals choose to undergo medical treatments or surgeries. Gender identity is a complex and personal matter, and there is no one right way to express it.

Some people may also identify as non-binary or genderqueer, meaning they do not exclusively identify as male or female. These identities fall under the broader umbrella of transgender, as they do not conform to the traditional binary of male and female.

In recent years, there has been more awareness and acceptance surrounding gender identity and expression. However, there is still a long way to go in terms of understanding and accepting the diversity within the transgender community.

It is crucial to remember that using the correct terminology and respecting a person's self-identification is essential in creating a more inclusive and supportive environment for transgender individuals.

In conclusion, transvestite, transgender, and transsexual are terms that refer to different aspects of gender identity. Transvestite refers to self-expression through clothing, transgender refers to a misalignment between gender identity and assigned sex, and transsexual refers to individuals who have undergone medical treatments to align their physical body with their gender identity. Remember to use the correct terminology and show respect and acceptance towards all gender identities.

Insights into the experiences of LGBTQ+ individuals in dating and relationships.

As a member of the LGBTQ+ community, navigating the world of dating and relationships can be a challenging and often confusing experience. From the constant fear of judgment and discrimination to the struggle of finding acceptance and understanding, there are many unique insights into the experiences of LGBTQ+ individuals in the dating scene.

One of the most common struggles for LGBTQ+ individuals is the fear of coming out and being open about their sexuality or gender identity. This fear often stems from the societal stigma and discrimination that still exists towards the LGBTQ+ community. Many LGBTQ+ individuals have experienced rejection and even violence because of their identity, making it difficult to trust others and be open about their true selves.

When it comes to dating, LGBTQ+ individuals

often face challenges in finding potential partners. In a heteronormative society, the dating pool is largely limited to those who identify as cisgender and heterosexual. This can make it challenging for LGBTQ+ individuals to find suitable partners, leading to feelings of isolation and loneliness. Additionally, many dating apps and websites are not inclusive of the LGBTQ+ community, further limiting their options.

In relationships, LGBTQ+ individuals often face different challenges compared to their heterosexual counterparts. For example, they may struggle with societal pressures and expectations about what a 'normal' relationship should look like. This can lead to anxiety and self-doubt, as they may feel like they are not living up to societal standards.

Furthermore, communication can be a significant challenge in LGBTQ+ relationships. Many individuals are still learning and exploring their identity, and this can make it difficult to openly communicate with their partner about their needs and boundaries. This can lead to misunderstandings and conflicts, as well as a lack of support and understanding from their significant other.

One particular issue that LGBTQ+ individuals face in their relationships is the lack of legal recognition and protection for their partnerships. In many countries, same-sex marriage is still not legal, which can make it difficult for LGBTQ+ couples to receive the same rights and benefits as heterosexual couples. This can create significant financial, legal, and emotional hurdles for LGBTQ+ individuals in relationships.

Despite these challenges, there are also many positive experiences that LGBTQ+ individuals can encounter in dating and relationships. Being a part of a marginalized community can bring a sense of unity and understanding between partners, as they both face similar struggles and can empathize with each other. There is also often a deep level of acceptance and authenticity within LGBTQ+ relationships, as both partners are free to be their true selves without fear of judgment or rejection.

In the end, the experiences of LGBTQ+ individuals in dating and relationships are complex and varied. While there are undoubtedly many challenges and obstacles to overcome, there is also love, support, and understanding within the community. As society continues to grow and evolve towards inclusivity and acceptance, we can hope that the experiences of LGBTQ+ individuals in dating and relationships will continue to improve and be filled with love and happiness.

Discussion on gender dysphoria and the importance of understanding one's gender identity.

Have you ever felt like you were born in the wrong body? Like you don't fully identify with the gender assigned to you at birth? If so, then you may have experienced gender dysphoria, a term used to describe the distress or discomfort one may feel due to a mismatch between their gender identity and assigned gender at birth. This topic has gained much attention in recent years, but it is not a new concept. Gender dysphoria has been a part of human experience for centuries and has been a source of confusion and discrimination. It is important to understand and respect the complexities of gender identity for individuals who experience this condition.

First, it is crucial to understand that gender identity is not the same as biological sex. Biological sex is determined by reproductive organs and hormones, while gender identity is an individual's deeply felt sense of being male, female, or a different gender altogether. For individuals with gender dysphoria, their emotional and psychological knowing of their gender does not match their physical body. It can cause intense distress and discomfort, leading individuals to experience depression, anxiety, and in extreme cases, even suicide.

The experience of gender dysphoria is unique to each individual. Some may feel that they are in the wrong body since childhood, while others may not realize it until later in life. It is a complex and personal journey that requires understanding and acceptance from both oneself and others. Unfortunately, societal norms and expectations often dictate what is considered 'normal' when it comes to gender identity. This can lead to rejection and discrimination towards those who don't fit into the binary of male and female.

It is crucial to understand that gender identity is a spectrum and not a binary. There are many variations of gender identities, such as non-binary, transgender, genderqueer, and genderfluid. Each person's journey is valid and deserves to be respected, even if it challenges traditional societal views. It is essential to create a safe and inclusive environment for individuals with gender dysphoria to feel accepted and supported.

Ignoring or denying one's gender identity can have severe consequences. It can lead to individuals suppressing their true selves, causing depression, anxiety, and feelings of isolation. It is why it is crucial for society to understand and acknowledge the complexities of gender identity and support those who identify differently from the gender they were assigned at birth.

One way to show support is by using the correct pronouns for individuals with gender dysphoria. This may seem like a small act, but it can mean the world to someone struggling with their gender identity. It is essential to educate ourselves and learn how to use the correct pronouns and avoid making assumptions about someone's gender identity.

Moreover, it is crucial to recognize that gender dysphoria is not a mental disorder. It is a natural expression of human diversity, and there is no one-size-fits-all solution. The process of transitioning, whether socially, medically, or both, is unique to each individual and can be a long and challenging journey. It is essential to provide support and understanding, rather than judgment and discrimination.

In conclusion, gender dysphoria is a complex and personal experience that requires understanding and acceptance from oneself and society. It is not a choice or a phase, but a fundamental aspect of an individual's identity. By acknowledging and respecting one's gender identity, we can create a more inclusive and compassionate world for individuals with gender dysphoria to thrive in. Let us all educate ourselves and be allies to those who are brave enough to embrace their true selves.

Chapter 6

Biromantic Asexuality and Beyond

You have always known that you were different. Growing up, you never quite understood the fascination your friends had with crushes and dating. While they were talking about their latest crush or swooning over a new celebrity heartthrob, you were more interested in reading a good book or spending time with your hobbies. You never felt any romantic or sexual attraction towards anyone, and for the longest time, you thought there was something wrong with you.

But then you stumbled upon the term 'asexuality' and it all suddenly made sense. Asexuality is defined as a lack of sexual attraction towards anyone. It is a spectrum, with some asexual individuals experiencing little to no sexual desire, while others experience it only under certain circumstances or towards certain people. While this discovery helped you understand yourself better, it still didn't fully explain your experience. That's when you learned about biromantic asexuality.

Biromantic asexuality is a specific identity within the asexual spectrum. It describes someone who is romantically attracted to both men and women but has little to no sexual desire towards them. You realized that this was exactly how you felt - you could develop deep emotional connections with both men and women, but the idea of engaging in sexual activity made you feel uncomfortable.

It was as if a weight had been lifted off your shoulders. Finally, there was a word to describe your experience and a community of people who understood and accepted you. But as you delved deeper into biromantic asexuality, you discovered that there was more to it than just the label. There was a whole world of experiences and challenges that came with being biromantic asexual.

One of the most significant challenges you

faced was breaking away from the societal norms and expectations of relationships. You had always been told that romantic and sexual relationships were the ultimate goal in life. But as a biromantic asexual, you didn't fit into that narrative. It was hard to explain to others that you were content with deep emotional connections and didn't need physical intimacy to feel fulfilled in a relationship.

You also had to navigate the world of dating, and it wasn't always easy. While some people were understanding and accepting of your identity, others were dismissive or even hostile. As if struggling with your own identity wasn't challenging enough, now you had to deal with others' ignorance and prejudices. But you didn't let it stop you from being true to yourself.

Through it all, you learned to embrace your biromantic asexuality and all the complexities that came with it. You realized that it was a beautiful and valid identity, just like any other. And while it may have been different from mainstream society's norms, it was your truth, and that's all that mattered.

But your journey didn't stop there. With further research and exploration, you discovered that there were even more diverse identities within the asexual spectrum. You learned about demisexuals, who experienced sexual attraction only after forming a strong emotional bond with someone, and gray asexuals, who fell somewhere in between asexual and sexual orientations. In the past, you may have felt alone and misunderstood, but now you felt like a part of a diverse and vibrant community.

Today, you proudly embrace your biromantic asexuality and your journey to self-discovery. You have come a long way from feeling like there was something wrong with you to living your truth and finding acceptance and understanding within yourself and from those around you. Your identity as a biromantic asexual is unique, and it has its challenges, but it is a part of who you are, and you wouldn't have it any other way.

In-depth exploration of asexuality and its place within the LGBTQ+ spectrum.

You've always known that you were different, but growing up in a world where your identity is constantly labeled and prescribed by society can make it hard to truly understand and embrace who you are. As a young member of the LGBTQ+ community, you may have struggled with happy and proud moments of self-acceptance, mixed with times of confusion and self-doubt. And as the world continues to evolve and conversations about identity and self-discovery grow louder, you may have found yourself questioning where you fit in and how to navigate your identity in a society that often reduces individuals to labels.

One aspect of the LGBTQ+ spectrum that often goes overlooked or misunderstood is asexuality. Asexuality, or the lack of sexual attraction to any gender, is a complex and diverse identity that is slowly gaining recognition within the LGBTQ+ community. In the past, asexuality was often dismissed as a phase or seen as a result of past trauma or emotional issues. But as more research and understanding is brought to the forefront, it is clear that asexuality is a valid identity that should be celebrated and embraced.

At first, you might have felt isolated and alone in your asexual identity. But you soon realized that you were not alone. Asexual individuals can be found in all races, genders, and sexual orientations, making it a nuanced and diverse identity within the LGBTQ+ spectrum. As you began to explore and understand your asexuality, you began to find a sense of belonging and connection to a community of individuals who shared similar experiences and struggles.

But navigating your asexuality within the LGBTQ+ community can often be challenging. While the community aims to be inclusive and accepting, there is still a lack of understanding and representation when it comes to asexuality. It can be hard to find your place and feel fully embraced within a community that is often centered around sexual and romantic relationships. But as society continues to break down harmful stereotypes and expand its understanding of sexuality, the asexual community is demanding visibility and acceptance within the LGBTQ+ community.

One of the most empowering aspects of embracing your asexuality is the freedom from societal expectations and pressures. In a world that is often obsessed with labeling and categorizing individuals based on their sexual orientation, being asexual challenges these norms and allows individuals to define their own experiences and desires. As you begin to understand and accept your asexuality, you realize that being happy and fulfilled does not have to revolve around societal expectations of love and romance. You are able to reject the narrative that links the importance of sexual relationships to a person's worth and find joy in other aspects of your life.

But as society continues to push for acceptance and understanding of asexuality, there are still stigmas and challenges that asexual individuals may face. A lack of representation in media and education can lead to a lack of understanding and even discrimination from those who do not understand or accept asexuality. It can also be challenging to navigate relationships with non-asexual individuals who may not fully understand or respect your identity.

However, despite these challenges, the asexual community continues to grow and thrive. As more individuals embrace and celebrate their asexuality, the community becomes stronger and more visible, making it easier for future generations to understand and accept this diverse identity within the LGBTQ+ spectrum.

In the end, being asexual is not something to be ashamed of, but rather something to be proud of and celebrated. Your asexuality is just one aspect of your identity, and it does not define who you are as a person. Embracing your asexuality and finding your place within the LGBTQ+ community not only empowers you but also contributes to a more diverse and inclusive society. As we continue to break down barriers and challenge societal norms, let us remember to embrace and celebrate the beautiful complexity of all identities, including asexuality.

Recognition of the diverse range of identities within the community and the importance of inclusivity.

As you walk down the bustling streets, you can feel a sense of joy emanating from within you. You are proud of who you are and your place in the world. You are part of the LGBTQ+ community, a diverse and vibrant community that celebrates love and identity in all forms. In today's world, where everyone strives to fit into labels and conform to societal norms, being proud of one's true self is a bold and radical act. But for you, it is second nature, because you have conquered confidence in a world obsessed with labels.

As you reflect on your journey, you remember the struggles you have faced as a member of the LGBTQ+ community. Growing up, you were constantly bombarded with societal expectations and rigid gender norms. You felt out of place, like you didn't fit into the predetermined boxes that society had set for you. It wasn't until you found a community of like-minded individuals that you realized you were not alone. This realization was empowering, and it gave you the strength to truly explore and embrace your identity.

One of the most beautiful things about the LGBTQ+ community is its diversity. Within this community, there is a vast spectrum of identities, each unique and valid in its own way. From gay, lesbian, bisexual, transgender, queer, intersex, asexual, and many more, the list goes on. This diversity is a celebration of individuality and reminds us that there is no one right way to be. It also serves as a reminder to constantly educate ourselves and be open to learning about new identities, even within the LGBTQ+ community.

Inclusivity is at the heart of the LGBTQ+ community, and it is crucial in ensuring that everyone feels seen, heard, and accepted. As you have navigated your own identity, you have also learned the importance of inclusivity. You understand that it is not enough to just accept your own identity; you must also advocate for and support others in their journey. As the saying goes, 'none of us are free until all of us are.'

Society often tries to put a label on everything and everyone, but the LGBTQ+ community is a rebellion against that notion. To be proud is to defy societal expectations and embrace your true self unapologetically. It is a journey of self-discovery and self-love that requires immense courage and strength. This is why the recognition of diverse identities within the LGBTQ+ community is so important. It gives individuals the permission to be who they are, without the fear of judgment or rejection.

But being proud and confident in a world obsessed with labels is not always easy. From discrimination and hate crimes to subtle forms of homophobia and transphobia, the LGBTQ+ community still faces many challenges. However, the resilience and spirit of this community are unbreakable. Together, you continue to fight for equality, visibility, and acceptance.

As you stand tall and proud, you can't help but feel a sense of gratitude for the individuals who have paved the way before you. The LGBTQ+ individuals who stood up and fought for their rights, who refused to be silenced, and who showed the world that love knows no boundaries. They are the reason you can walk with your head held high and be celebrated for who you are.

In conclusion, the LGBTQ+ community is a diverse and inclusive community that celebrates love, identity, and individuality. It serves as a reminder that we are all unique and beautiful in our own way, and we should be proud to express our true selves. As you continue to navigate your journey, remember to be kind, compassionate, and inclusive towards others. Your voice and your story have the power to inspire others and create a world where everyone can be proud and confident in their identity.

Promoting understanding and acceptance of all sexual and gender identities.

You stand tall and proud, walking down the streets with confidence radiating from your every step. You are a member of the LGBTQ+ community, and you wear your identity like a badge of honor. It wasn't always this way - you've had your fair share of struggles, doubts, and fears. But today, you embrace who you are and take pride in your unique identity.

But living in a world that is obsessed with labels

can make it challenging to fully accept and love yourself. From a young age, society has taught us to conform to strict gender and sexual norms, leaving no room for anyone who falls outside of these predefined categories. As a result, the LGBTQ+ community has suffered from discrimination, violence, and a lack of understanding.

But times are changing, and with more visibility and representation, the world is slowly becoming a more accepting and inclusive place for all sexual and gender identities. And you, as a proud member of the community, have a crucial role to play in promoting understanding and acceptance of all sexual and gender identities.

The first and most crucial step is to start within yourself. It can be a hard and scary process to come to terms with your unique identity, but accepting and loving yourself is the foundation for promoting understanding and acceptance. Embrace your identity and be unapologetic about who you are. You have the power to be a role model for others who may be struggling with their own identity.

Education and awareness are also essential in promoting understanding and acceptance. As a member of the LGBTQ+ community, you have an intimate understanding of the struggles and challenges that come with your identity. By sharing your story and experiences, you can help educate others and break down harmful stereotypes and misconceptions. The more individuals are exposed to the diverse perspectives and experiences of the community, the more accepting and understanding they will become.

Seek out opportunities to engage in conversations and discussions about LGBTQ+ issues. Whether it's with friends, family, or coworkers, open and honest communication is key in promoting understanding and breaking down barriers. By sharing your personal experiences, you can humanize the LGBTQ+ community and make people see beyond labels and see the person behind the identity.

Support and allyship are also crucial in promoting understanding and acceptance. As a member of the community, you know how much it means to have someone stand by your side and advocate for your rights and equality. Use your voice to speak up for not only yourself but also for others in the community. Support LGBTQ+ organizations, attend pride events, and show your love and acceptance for all sexual and gender identities.

And finally, never underestimate the power of small acts of kindness and compassion. Whether it's a smile, a hug, or a simple word of encouragement, these small gestures can have a significant impact on someone who may be struggling with their identity. Show compassion and understanding towards those who may not fully understand or accept the LGBTQ+ community. Your kindness can plant seeds of change in their minds and hearts.

Promoting understanding and acceptance of all sexual and gender identities starts with you. By embracing and loving yourself, educating others, engaging in meaningful conversations, and showing support and allyship, you can make a difference in promoting a more inclusive and accepting world. Keep being proud of who you are, and never stop fighting for equality and acceptance. Your story and your voice matter. Together, we can conquer the world's obsession with labels and promote a world where all sexual and gender identities are celebrated and accepted.

Chapter 7

Coming Out, Self-Exploration, Empowerment, and Embracing Pride

You've spent most of your life feeling like you didn't quite fit in. You had always known that you were different, but it wasn't until you reached your teenage years that you started to realize just how different you were. As you navigated through high school and into early adulthood, you struggled to understand your true identity and where you belonged in the world.

It took a lot of courage and self-exploration, but you finally came to terms with your true self – you are a member of the LGBTQ+ community. For many, this realization is both terrifying and liberating, and it often leads to a journey of self-discovery, acceptance, and empowerment. And while it may seem daunting at first, coming out and embracing your identity can be a truly rewarding and fulfilling experience.

Coming out is a pivotal moment in the LGBTQ+ community. It is a deeply personal and individual process, and no two experiences are the same. For some, it might be a sudden revelation, while for others, it may be a gradual acceptance of their true identity. Regardless of how it happens, coming out can be an emotional rollercoaster filled with fear, anxiety, and uncertainty.

But with the right support and resources, coming out can also be a source of immense joy and pride. It's the moment when you finally shed the weight of hiding your true self and step into your authentic identity. It's a powerful act of self-love and self-acceptance, and it takes immense courage to do so. So, if you're struggling with the idea of coming out, know that you are not alone, and it's okay to take your time until you feel ready.

As you continue on your journey, you'll also

embark on a path of self-exploration. This is the time to explore all aspects of your identity – your gender, your sexuality, and everything in between. It's about discovering what truly makes you happy and embracing it with open arms. It's also a time to surround yourself with a supportive community that celebrates and embraces the beautiful diversity within the LGBTQ+ community.

Through self-exploration, you'll gain a deeper understanding of your identity and learn how to embrace it with pride. It's a process that requires patience, vulnerability, and a willingness to challenge societal norms and expectations. But as you delve deeper into your true self, you'll also begin to feel a sense of empowerment.

Self-empowerment is an essential aspect of LGBTQ+ identity. It's about owning your true self, regardless of what labels society may try to impose on you. It's about embracing your uniqueness and understanding that you are enough, exactly as you are. And while it may not be easy, self-empowerment is a powerful tool that can help you overcome any obstacles that come your way.

Finally, as you continue on your journey, you'll learn the importance of embracing your pride. Pride goes beyond just a month-long celebration – it's a way of life. It's about recognizing and celebrating the struggles and triumphs of the LGBTQ+ community and continuing to fight for equality and acceptance. It's also about being unapologetically yourself and inspiring others to do the same.

In a world that is often obsessed with labels and fitting into societal norms, the journey towards self-discovery and embracing pride can be challenging. But know that you are not alone, and your identity is something to be proud of. It's a beautiful and unique part of who you are, and it deserves to be celebrated and embraced. So, keep exploring, empowering, and being proud of who you are – for that is the true essence of your LGBTQ+ identity.

Addressing the process of questioning one's identity

As you sit in front of your computer, scrolling through the endless feeds of social media, a sudden thought crosses your mind – "Who am I?". You pause for a moment, mulling over this question, a question that many of us have asked ourselves at some point in our lives. But for you, this question holds much more weight. It is a question of identity, a question that has been constantly nagging and tugging at your heart for as long as you can remember. The question of your LGBTQ+ identity.

Growing up, you always felt like you were different from those around you. You couldn't quite put your finger on it, but you knew that you didn't fit into the "norms" of society. As you watch your friends effortlessly navigate through their gender and sexuality, you can't help but feel lost and confused. Questions pop into your head – "Am I really gay?", "Do I identify as cisgender?", "What does it even mean to be transgender?" – and the list goes on. The process of questioning your identity can be a daunting and overwhelming experience, but know that you are not alone.

In today's world, where we are constantly bombarded with labels and societal expectations, it is easy to get lost in the process of trying to understand and define ourselves. Society has a way of putting people into neat little boxes, but the truth is, our identities are complex and cannot be confined by these labels. As you try to make sense of your own identity, it is important to remember that it is okay to not have all the answers right away. The journey of self-discovery is a lifelong process, and it is perfectly normal to constantly question and re-evaluate your identity.

It is also important to acknowledge that there is no one "right" way to identify within the LGBTQ+ community. We often feel pressured to choose a specific label and conform to it, but the truth is, sexuality and gender exist on a spectrum. You may identify as one thing today and something else tomorrow, and that is perfectly valid. The most important thing is to be true to yourself and embrace your ever-evolving identity.

However, the process of questioning your identity can also come with its own set of challenges. You may face backlash from society, discrimination, and even internalized homophobia or transphobia. These challenges can take a toll on your mental health and self-confidence. But remember, you are not defined by these challenges, and they do not diminish the beauty and strength of your identity.

One way to find strength and confidence in your identity is by seeking support and connection within the LGBTQ+ community. Connecting with others who share similar experiences and identities can be empowering and reassuring. You may also find solace in talking to friends or family members who are accepting and understanding. Surrounding yourself with a positive support system can help you feel confident and proud of who you are.

In the end, the journey of questioning your identity is a personal one, and there is no one-size-fits-all approach. Embrace your uniqueness, explore your identity with an open mind, and know that there is no "right" way to be LGBTQ+. Trust yourself, trust your journey, and you will find joy and pride in your identity.

So, as you continue scrolling through your social media feeds, remember that you are more than just a label. You are a beautiful, complex, and ever-evolving person with a unique LGBTQ+ identity. Embrace every part of yourself, and always remember to be proud of who you are. It is that confidence and self-acceptance that will help you conquer any obstacles and thrive in a world obsessed with labels.

Overcoming challenges faced when coming out

Coming out as a member of the LGBTQ+ community is a deeply personal and often challenging experience. Whether you are lesbian, gay, bisexual, transgender, queer, or any other identity, the process of revealing your true self to others can be fraught with fear, uncertainty, and even rejection. However, overcoming these challenges and fully embracing your identity can also bring immense joy, pride, and newfound confidence.

You may have always known deep down that you were different from your peers. Perhaps you felt more drawn to people of the same gender, or you didn't feel comfortable conforming to traditional notions of gender roles. Maybe you struggled with feelings of shame and confusion, unsure of who you were or where you belonged.

But as you grew older, you began to explore and understand your identity more deeply. You found comfort and support in online communities and queer-affirming spaces, and you slowly gained the courage to come out to the people in your life. You took the first step towards living your truth and embracing your LGBTQ+ identity.

However, the coming out process is not always easy. You may have faced resistance and discrimination from family members, friends, and even society at large. The fear of rejection and judgment can be overwhelming, and it takes a great deal of strength to continue on this journey.

One of the most significant challenges you may have faced while coming out is the pressure to conform to societal norms and labels. Our society is obsessed with putting things into neat little boxes, and this is especially true when it comes to sexuality and gender identity. This constant need to label and categorize can be suffocating for those within the LGBTQ+ community. Suddenly, you are expected to fit into a certain label and conform to rigid expectations, rather than being allowed to express yourself authentically.

This pressure to conform can be especially hard for transgender individuals. Society often imposes strict gender roles and expectations, making it difficult for individuals to fully embrace their gender identity. This not only adds an extra layer of difficulty to the coming out process but also can lead to feelings of isolation and shame.

However, it is essential to remember that your identity is valid regardless of what others may say. You do not have to fit into any specific label or conform to societal norms to be accepted or feel proud of who you are. You are unique, and that is something to be celebrated and embraced.

Overcoming these challenges and fully embracing your LGBTQ+ identity also involves overcoming internalized homophobia and transphobia. Growing up in a society that often rejects and stigmatizes diversity can lead to feelings of self-hatred and shame. This internal struggle can be one of the most challenging obstacles to overcome when coming out.

But as you continue on this journey of self-discovery, surrounded by a supportive community, you will slowly start to shed these negative beliefs. You will learn to love and accept yourself for who you are, unapologetically and proudly.

In the end, the challenges you face when coming out as LGBTQ+ will only make you stronger. They will shape you into a resilient and confident individual, ready to stand tall and conquer any obstacle in your path. And as you continue to explore and navigate your identity in a world obsessed with labels, always remember that your pride and joy come from within, not from societal norms or expectations. You are living your truth, and that is something to be celebrated. Stay true to yourself, and you will find happiness and confidence in your identity.

Exploring asexuality and nonbinary topics

You have always known that you were different. While your friends gushed over romantic relationships and crushes, you couldn't seem to understand the hype. You never felt the need to conform to society's expectations of love and attraction. You always thought there was something wrong with you, until you discovered asexuality and nonbinary identities.

Exploring asexuality and nonbinary topics can be a challenge , especially in a world obsessed with labels and societal norms. But it is a journey worth undertaking, as it leads to a deeper understanding and acceptance of yourself.

Firstly, let's break down the concept of asexuality. It is often misunderstood as having no interest in sex at all, when in reality, it refers to a lack of sexual attraction. Asexual individuals can still have romantic and emotional connections with others, without experiencing sexual desire. This is just one aspect of asexuality, as it encompasses a spectrum of identities, including demisexuality (feeling sexual attraction only after forming a strong emotional connection with someone) and graysexuality (experiencing limited sexual attraction).

Discovering your asexuality can be liberating, as it validates your feelings and experiences. You may have felt broken or abnormal for not fitting into society's expectations of sexuality, but now you understand that there is nothing wrong with you. You simply have a different way of experiencing the world.

However, this can also be a difficult realization to come to terms with. You may face skepticism or even rejection from those who do not understand asexuality. People may question the validity of your identity and try to label you as 'broken' or 'prudish.' This is where the journey of acceptance and self-love begins.

Similar to asexuality, being nonbinary challenges societal norms. It refers to individuals who do not identify as strictly male or female, and instead, fall somewhere in between or outside of the gender binary. This can involve using nonbinary pronouns (such as they/them) and rejecting gendered expectations and roles.

Navigating the world as a nonbinary person can be overwhelming. From filling out forms that only offer 'male' or 'female' options, to being misgendered and invalidated by those around you, it can feel like you are constantly fighting against a system that refuses to acknowledge your existence.

But as you look deeper into your nonbinary identity, you will realize that it is not about fitting into a box, but rather, rejecting the idea of boxes altogether. You are not confined to society's narrow definitions of gender and can express yourself however you please. It is a powerful and liberating feeling, to live your authentic truth and to defy the limitations imposed by society.

While exploring asexuality and nonbinary topics may come with its challenges, it also opens up a whole new world of understanding and acceptance. It allows you to break free from the constraints of labels and expectations, and to embrace your true self. Along this journey, you will also discover a diverse and supportive community, who will celebrate and validate your identity.

In a world obsessed with labels, it's easy to feel lost and isolated when you do not fit into the norm. But by embracing your asexuality and nonbinary identity, you are paving the way for others to do the same. You are a trailblazer, redefining what it means to be proud of one's identity in today's world.

So embrace your asexuality and nonbinary identity with confidence and pride. You are not alone, and your journey of self-discovery and acceptance is a beautiful and unique experience. Remember, your identity is valid, and it is yours to define, regardless of what society may tell you. Keep exploring and conquering the world with your authentic self.

Tips for navigating relationships and dating as an LGBTQ+ individual

Growing up in a society that is obsessed with labels can be challenging, especially when it comes to relationships and dating. As a member of the LGBTQ+ community, you have probably faced your fair share of struggles and hurdles in finding love and acceptance. With society constantly trying to put you in a box and define your identity, it can be overwhelming to navigate the dating scene. But do not be afraid , because there are ways to conquer these challenges and find love and happiness as an LGBTQ+ individual.

1. Know and embrace your identity

The first step to navigate relationships and dating as an LGBTQ+ individual is to know and embrace your identity. It is essential to understand and be confident in who you are and what you want. This will not only help you in finding a partner who shares the same values, but it will also help you filter out those who do not understand or accept your identity. Embracing your identity also means being proud of it and not letting anyone make you feel ashamed or inferior because of it.

2. Educate yourself and your partner

It is essential to educate yourself and your partner about the LGBTQ+ community. This can help you understand each other's perspectives and create a safe and accepting environment for your relationship. It is also vital to educate yourself on important LGBTQ+ issues, such as discrimination and inequality, so that you can be an ally to your partner and the community as a whole.

3. Don't settle for less

As an LGBTQ+ person, you might feel pressured to settle for less, especially in a society that promotes heteronormative relationships. But remember, you deserve to be treated with love and respect, just like anyone else. Do not settle for a partner who is not willing to accept and embrace your identity fully. You should be with someone who loves and supports you for who you are.

4. Be open and honest

Honesty is crucial in any relationship, especially when it comes to LGBTQ+ relationships. Be open and honest with your partner about your identity, your past experiences, and your expectations for the future. This will not only build trust but also create a strong and healthy foundation for your relationship.

5. Seek support from the LGBTQ+ community

Navigating relationships and dating can be challenging, but it can be even more challenging if you feel like you are doing it alone. That is why it is important to seek support from the LGBTQ+ community. Join online forums, attend events, and make connections with other LGBTQ+ individuals. You can also seek out LGBTQ+-friendly therapists or support groups, which can be extremely beneficial for your mental and emotional well-being.

6. Be patient

Patience is key when it comes to relationships, especially as an LGBTQ+ individual. You might face rejection and discrimination, but remember that it is not a reflection of who you are, but rather of their narrow-mindedness. Be patient, and know that the right person will come along at the right time.

In conclusion, navigating relationships and

dating as an LGBTQ+ individual can be a challenging journey, but it is not impossible. Remember to know and embrace your identity, educate yourself and your partner, and be open and honest in your relationships. Seek support from the LGBTQ+ community, and most importantly, be patient. You deserve love and happiness, and with these tips, you can conquer any obstacles and find the fulfilling relationship you deserve.

Providing resources and support for LGBTQ+ individuals

As you walk down the street holding your partner's hand, you can't help but feel a sense of fear and uncertainty. Will someone yell a homophobic slur at you? Will you be denied a job or a service because of your sexual orientation or gender identity? These are just a few of the constant fears and struggles that many LGBTQ+ individuals face on a daily basis.

Fortunately, there are resources and support

systems in place that can help you navigate through these challenges and empower you to live your life authentically and proudly. These resources and support are crucial in creating a safe and inclusive environment for the LGBTQ+ community.

One of the most essential resources is community organizations and centers. These organizations provide a safe and welcoming space for LGBTQ+ individuals to gather, share experiences, and support one another. They also offer a variety of services such as counseling, educational workshops, and social events that promote a sense of belonging and unity within the community.

You may also find comfort and support through online communities and forums. These virtual spaces allow you to connect with other LGBTQ+ individuals from all over the world, share your story, and receive advice and encouragement from those who have been through similar experiences.

In addition to community organizations and online communities, there are also numerous hotlines and helplines available for LGBTQ+ individuals to access emotional support and resources. These hotlines are often staffed by trained volunteers who are ready to listen and provide guidance in times of need.

Furthermore, many healthcare providers now offer specialized care for LGBTQ+ individuals. From gender-affirming hormone therapy to mental health services, these providers understand the unique needs and challenges that the community may face and are equipped to provide the necessary support and resources.

In recent years, there has also been a growing number of corporations and businesses that have taken steps to support the LGBTQ+ community. From offering diversity and inclusion training to providing health benefits for LGBTQ+ employees, these companies are making efforts to create a more inclusive and supportive workplace for all individuals regardless of their sexual orientation or gender identity.

Moreover, there are countless advocacy and legal organizations fighting for LGBTQ+ rights and providing legal assistance for discrimination cases. These organizations are crucial in protecting the rights and ensuring the safety of the community, and their services are often free of charge.

It is important to remember that you are not alone and that there is always help and support available to you. Whether it's seeking out a community organization, reaching out to an online forum, or simply making a call to a hotline, there are resources out there that can empower you to be your true self and live without fear or discrimination.

Never be afraid to ask for help or seek support because in doing so, you are not only helping yourself but also building a stronger and more inclusive community for future generations. Stay strong, and know that you are loved and accepted just the way you are.

Encouraging pride and self-acceptance within the community

You are a part of the LGBTQ+ community, a community that is constantly evolving and facing challenges in today's world. You may have at some point struggled with finding pride in your identity, surrounded by a society that is obsessed with labels and binaries. But let me tell you, your identity is not something that needs to be labeled or defined by anyone else. It is a fluid and beautiful part of you that should be celebrated and embraced with pride.

The journey towards self-acceptance and pride within the LGBTQ+ community can often be a difficult one. There are societal pressures to conform to traditional gender roles and expectations, leading to feelings of shame and self-doubt. But who is to say that these norms are the only ones that define us? It is time to break free from these labels and explore our identities in all their complexities.

One of the most important steps towards encouraging pride and self-acceptance within the community is to surround ourselves with people who support and uplift us. This can be our chosen family, friends, or even online communities. They provide a safe and accepting space where we can freely express ourselves without any fear of judgment. These supportive relationships are crucial in boosting our confidence and helping us navigate through our journey towards self-love and acceptance.

Another crucial factor in cultivating pride within the community is representation. The media often portrays LGBTQ+ individuals in a negative light, perpetuating harmful stereotypes. This can lead to feelings of shame and inadequacy within the community. But when we see positive and diverse representation of our community in media and pop culture, it not only helps us feel seen and heard, but it also promotes a sense of acceptance and pride. It is important for us to amplify and celebrate these voices and stories within our community.

It is also essential for us to remember that our identities are not static. We are constantly evolving and growing, and so is our understanding of our identities. It is okay to not fit into societal norms and expectations. Embrace your uniqueness and explore your identity, free from the pressures of labels and binaries. Celebrate every aspect of yourself and know that you are valid and worthy of love and acceptance.

Moreover, pride and self-acceptance within the LGBTQ+ community can also be fostered by advocating for and supporting each other. We are a diverse community with unique experiences and struggles, but we are all in this together. Let us uplift and empower each other, and break the barriers of discrimination and prejudice. By standing together, we can create a world where our identities are celebrated, not judged.

In a world that is constantly trying to label and categorize us, it can be challenging to find pride and confidence in our identities. But by embracing our uniqueness and supporting each other, we can conquer these challenges and shine with pride. Remember, your identity is something to be celebrated, not hidden. Let us conquer the world with our pride and show the world that we are here, we are queer, and we are proud.

Promoting activism and advocacy for LGBTQ+ rights

Are you proud of who you are? As a member of the LGBTQ+ community, it may have been a long journey to reach a place of self-acceptance and confidence. But now that you have found your identity, it is important to use your voice and platform to promote activism and advocacy for LGBTQ+ rights. In today's world, where society is still obsessed with labels and traditional norms, it's crucial to continuously fight for equality and acceptance for all.

It's not an easy task, but your identity and your unique experiences give you a perspective that is vital in promoting change. As an LGBTQ+ individual, you understand the struggles and challenges faced by the community every day. Your experiences have shaped you into a strong and resilient person, and it's time to use that strength to make a difference.

One of the most effective ways to promote activism and advocacy for LGBTQ+ rights is through education and awareness. Many people still hold onto outdated and harmful beliefs about the community due to ignorance or lack of exposure. By sharing your story and educating others about the diversity and complexity of gender and sexuality, you can break down these barriers and show that LGBTQ+ individuals are just like everyone else.

You can also get involved in campaigns and

organizations that work towards promoting equality and fighting for LGBTQ+ rights. Volunteer your time, donate to causes that are important to you, and participate in events and demonstrations. It's crucial to show your support and be an active member of the community. The more people are willing to speak up, the stronger our collective voice becomes.

Another crucial aspect of promoting activism and advocacy for LGBTQ+ rights is to call out discrimination when you see it. It's not always easy, but staying silent means allowing bigotry and hate to continue. Use your voice to speak up against discrimination and hate speech, whether it's in your personal life or in the media. With each person who speaks out, the message becomes louder and clearer.

It's also important to remember that promoting activism doesn't always have to be on a large scale. You can make a difference in your everyday life by being a positive role model and advocate for equality. Show support for your

LGBTQ+ friends and family, and don't be afraid to stand up for yourself and others when faced with discrimination. Your words and actions can have a profound impact on those around you.

Lastly, it's essential to practice self-care and self-love in the midst of promoting activism and advocacy. It can be emotionally draining and overwhelming, but remember that taking care of yourself is crucial in order to continue fighting for the community. Surround yourself with supportive and understanding individuals, and don't be afraid to take a step back when needed.

In today's world, it's more important than ever to promote activism and advocacy for LGBTQ+ rights. As a proud member of the community, you have a unique perspective and voice that can make a difference. Whether through education, involvement, or everyday actions, you have the power to challenge societal norms and promote equality for all. Keep fighting, stay strong, and remember to always be proud of who you are.

Understanding the importance of embracing LGBTQ+ identity

You have always felt a little different from others. As a child, you were told that boys like blue and girls like pink, but you couldn't understand why you preferred purple. As you grew older, you started to realize that your attraction to the same gender went against societal norms and expectations. You were constantly bombarded with labels and stereotypes, and it made you feel like you didn't fit in. But then, you discovered the LGBTQ+ community and everything changed.

Embracing your LGBTQ+ identity is a powerful and liberating experience. It means accepting and loving yourself for who you truly are, without any apologies or excuses. It means being a part of a diverse and vibrant community that celebrates individuality and inclusivity. And most importantly, it means breaking free from the limitations that society has imposed on you.

But embracing your identity is not always easy, especially in a world that is still obsessed with labels and categories. You might have faced discrimination and prejudice, or even struggled with your own internalized homophobia or transphobia. You may have been told that you are not "normal" or that your identity is invalid. These kinds of messages can be damaging and hurtful, and they can make you question your own worth.

This is where the importance of embracing your LGBTQ+ identity comes into play. Embracing your identity means rejecting the negative messages and embracing the positive ones. It means rejecting the fear and stereotypes and embracing love and authenticity. It means finding the confidence to stand up tall and proud of who you are.

One of the biggest challenges that the LGBTQ+ community faces is the fear of coming out. The fear of rejection, discrimination, and judgement can be overwhelming. But by embracing your identity, you are taking the first step towards conquering that fear. When you embrace your identity, you are declaring to the world that you refuse to be defined by society's narrow definitions and expectations. You are showing that you will not hide or apologize for who you are.

Embracing your identity also means understanding the importance of visibility. By being open and proud of your identity, you are paving the way for others to do the same. You are being a role model for those who are still struggling to accept themselves. Your existence and visibility are crucial in the fight for LGBTQ+ rights and equality.

Moreover, embracing your LGBTQ+ identity also means finding a sense of community and belonging. The LGBTQ+ community is a diverse and beautiful family that is bound by a shared sense of understanding and acceptance. By embracing your identity, you are opening yourself up to a world of new friendships, experiences, and perspectives. You are no longer alone, because you have found a community that celebrates your uniqueness and loves you for who you are.

In a world that is constantly trying to label and categorize us, embracing our LGBTQ+ identity is an act of rebellion. It is a powerful statement that says we will not be confined by society's expectations. We are who we are, and we are proud of it. So, my dear reader, embrace your identity with all the joy and pride that it deserves. Embrace it with the understanding that it is a beautiful and integral part of who you are. And most importantly, embrace it with the courage and confidence to conquer a world that is still learning to accept and celebrate diversity.

Encouraging self-love and acceptance for all individuals within the community

You are a uniquely wonderful individual, with your own passions, beliefs, and identity. And part of that identity may include being a proud member of the LGBTQ+ community. In today's society, where labels and stereotypes seem to be everywhere, it can be easy to feel like you have to fit into a certain mold. But, my dear, let me tell you, you are not defined by any label. You are defined by your own beautiful, authentic self.

In a world where society often imposes narrow ideas of what it means to be 'normal,' those who identify as part of the LGBTQ+ community may struggle with fully embracing and loving themselves. But the truth is, there is no one way to be you. Your gender identity or sexual orientation does not limit or define who you are as a person. You are so much more than that.

It's time to break free from the pressure of fitting in and embrace your uniqueness. Celebrate your journey and your identity, regardless of what anyone else may say or think. Your self-love and acceptance is not dependent on anyone else's validation. It is something that comes from within, from embracing all aspects of yourself and knowing that you are worthy and deserving of love and happiness.

As part of the LGBTQ+ community, you may have faced discrimination or even rejection from those around you. But my dear, those experiences do not define you. They do not diminish your worth or your right to be happy. They do not take away from the fact that you are a strong, courageous and beautiful individual. And through all of the struggles, you have learned to love and accept yourself even more fiercely.

It's important to remember that self-love and acceptance isn't a one-time achievement. It's a continuous journey, one that you must actively choose every day. This means standing up for yourself and setting boundaries, whether it's with family, friends, or society as a whole. It means surrounding yourself with people who support and uplift you, and letting go of those who don't. It means embracing your own definition of happiness and not conforming to anyone else's expectations.

But my dear, it's not just about self-love and acceptance for yourself. It's also about extending that love and acceptance to others within the LGBTQ+ community. Every person has their own unique journey and experiences, and it's important to celebrate and respect those differences. We are all on this journey together, and together, we are stronger. So let's stand in solidarity, uplift and empower each other, and continue to break down the societal barriers that try to divide us.

Also, you are so much more than any label or stereotype. You are a proud member of the LGBTQ+ community, and your identity is something to be cherished and celebrated. Embrace all aspects of yourself, love and accept yourself unapologetically, and spread that love and acceptance to others. Remember, we all have the right to be proud, to be joyful, and to conquer our confidence. So go out into the world, confidently and unapologetically, knowing that you are loved and accepted just the way you are.

Emphasizing the value of unity and solidarity in the fight for LGBTQ+ equality

Standing at the center of the bustling Pride parade, surrounded by colorful flags, vibrant costumes, and jubilant voices, you can't help but feel a sense of unity and solidarity. In this moment, labels and differences fade away, and all that remains is the powerful message of love, acceptance, and equality. As a member or ally of the LGBTQ+ community, you know firsthand the importance of unity and solidarity in the fight for LGBTQ+ equality. But in a world so obsessed with labels, how can we emphasize the value of unity and solidarity in this ongoing battle?

In today's world, the LGBTQ+ community faces numerous challenges and obstacles. From discrimination and hate crimes to unequal rights and limited representation, the fight for LGBTQ+ equality is far from over. But amidst all of these struggles, one thing remains constant – the strength and resilience of the community. And it is this strength that is rooted in the value of unity and solidarity.

Unity is the coming together of individuals to form a cohesive whole. Solidarity is the support and cooperation among these individuals. Together, these two elements create a powerful force that can conquer any challenge. As a member of the LGBTQ+ community, you have experienced firsthand the power of unity and solidarity. You have seen how individuals from different backgrounds, with different identities, can come together under one common goal – to fight for LGBTQ+ equality.

But in a world that is divided by labels and differences, it can be a challenge to emphasize the value of unity and solidarity. Many within and outside the community may fall into the trap of categorizing and labeling individuals based on their sexual orientation, gender identity, or expression. This not only creates divisions within the community but also dilutes the message of equality and acceptance.

As you march in the Pride parade, you see a sea of diverse faces and hear a chorus of different voices. But instead of focusing on differences, you choose to celebrate the similarities. You see individuals who are proud to be who they are, who are fighting for a common cause, and who are united in their support for each other. You realize that the strength of the community lies in embracing these differences and standing together in solidarity.

To emphasize the value of unity and solidarity, we must first reject the obsession with labels. Rather than placing individuals into boxes, we should embrace the diversity within the community. We should celebrate the uniqueness of each individual and recognize that their differences are what make the community stronger.

Furthermore, we must also encourage and support initiatives that promote unity and solidarity. This can be done through events like Pride parades, where the community comes together to celebrate and advocate for equal rights. It can also be achieved through organizations and platforms that foster dialogue and cooperation within the community.

As you reach the end of the parade, you look back and see the trail of rainbows and glitter that showcases the vibrancy and diversity of the community. You are filled with a sense of pride and joy, knowing that you are a part of a community that values unity and solidarity. And as you continue your journey in this world, you carry with you the conviction that it is this unity and solidarity that will ultimately pave the way for LGBTQ+ equality.

Therefore , the fight for LGBTQ+ equality is a collective effort, and it is the value of unity and solidarity that will lead us towards victory. Let us stand together, embrace our differences, and continue to advocate for a world where all love is recognized and celebrated. After all, in a world that is so divided, the LGBTQ+ community provides a beacon of hope, resilience, and unwavering unity

Providing resources and support for LGBTQ+ individuals.

You are strong, you are brave, and you are proud. As an LGBTQ+ individual, you have faced your fair share of challenges, but through it all, your identity has only grown stronger. In a world that is still obsessed with labels and filled with discrimination, you have found the courage to be yourself and defy societal norms. Despite the obstacles, you have found joy in your identity and have embarked on a journey of self-discovery and self-love. Today, we are here to tell you that you are not alone. There is a whole community of individuals just like you who are ready to support and uplift you on your journey.

As you navigate through life, there may be times when you feel isolated and misunderstood. It is in those moments that having a support system becomes crucial. That is why it is essential to have resources and support readily available for individuals within the LGBTQ+ community. These resources range from helplines, support groups, online communities, and educational materials, all aimed at providing a safe and inclusive space for individuals to express themselves and seek guidance.

In today's world, with the rise of technology, it has become easier to access resources and connect with people from all over the world such as :

1. The Trevor Project: A leading national organization providing crisis intervention and suicide prevention services to LGBTQ+ young people under 25. They offer a 24/7 hotline, text, and chat services staffed by trained counselors.

Website: https://www.thetrevorproject.org/

2. GLAAD: A media advocacy organization promoting understanding, acceptance, and equality for LGBTQ+ individuals. They provide resources for media professionals and offer support for LGBTQ+ representation in media.

Website: https://www.glaad.org/

3. Human Rights Campaign (HRC): The largest LGBTQ+ civil rights organization in the United States, advocating for equality for LGBTQ+ people. HRC offers resources on coming out, workplace equality, healthcare, and more.

Website: https://www.hrc.org/

4. PFLAG (Parents, Families, and Friends of Lesbians and Gays): A nonprofit organization providing support, education, and advocacy for LGBTQ+ individuals and their families. PFLAG has chapters nationwide offering support meetings and resources.

Website: https://pflag.org/

5. LGBT National Help Center: Provides free and confidential peer support and resources for LGBTQ+ individuals. They offer hotlines, online chat, and email support, as well as specialized resources for youth, seniors, and Spanish speakers.

Website: https://www.glbthotline.org/

6. National Center for Transgender Equality (NCTE): Advocates for policy change to advance the equality of transgender people. They offer resources on issues such as identity documents, healthcare, and employment discrimination.

Website: https://transequality.org/

7. Trans Lifeline: A crisis hotline staffed by transgender people for transgender people, offering support and resources to those in crisis or in need of assistance.

Website: https://www.translifeline.org/

8. Local LGBTQ+ Community Centers: Many cities and towns have LGBTQ+ community centers that offer support groups, social events, counseling services, and resources specific to the local community. You can search online for centers near you.

9. The Gay, Lesbian & Straight Education Network (GLSEN): An organization that works to create safe and inclusive schools for LGBTQ students. GLSEN provides resources for educators, parents, and students.

 Remember, reaching out for support is a sign of strength, and there are people and organizations ready to support you. You are not alone, and there is a community that cares about you and your well-being.

These resources provide a safe space for individuals to express themselves, seek guidance, and find acceptance. As an LGBTQ+ individual, remember that you are not alone, and there is a community that supports and celebrates you for who you are. You are proud, you are joy, and you are a vital part of this world. Let your confidence shine, and continue to break free from those labels and stereotypes.

CONCLUSION

Overall, it is important to remember that your LGBTQ+ identity is something to be proud of. Despite the societal pressures to conform and fit into specific labels, it is crucial to stay true to yourself and embrace all aspects of your identity.

It may not always be easy, but conquering confidence in a world obsessed with labels will ultimately lead to a more fulfilling and authentic life. Remember to surround yourself with a supportive and accepting community, and never be afraid to speak your truth and stand up for what you believe in.

Celebrate your uniqueness and know that you are a valuable and important member of the LGBTQ+ community. Be proud, be confident, and always remember that you are not alone in your journey. The world is ever-changing, and your identity is valid and deserving of respect and acceptance.

Keep shining your light and living your truth, because there is nothing more empowering than being proud of who you are and embracing your LGBTQ+ identity. So go forth with pride, knowing that you are not alone. You are part of a vibrant and supportive community that celebrates diversity, champions equality, and stands united in the pursuit of a better, more inclusive world.

With each step you take, remember: You are worthy. You are valid. You are loved. And above all, you are joyfully, unapologetically, and proudly you.

Embrace your identity.

Embrace your journey. Embrace your joy.

Congratulations on your journey of self-discovery, and may your pride continue to shine brightly in all that you do.